C A P S T O N E

T0341592

Stay Smart!

Smart things to know about... is a complete library of the world's smartest business ideas. **Smart** books put you on the inside track to the knowledge and skills that make the most successful people tick.

Each book brings you right up to speed on a crucial business issue. The subjects that business people tell us they most want to master are:

Smart Things to Know about **Brands & Branding**, JOHN MARIOTTI

Smart Things to Know about **Business Finance**, KEN LANGDON

Smart Things to Know about **Change**, DAVID FIRTH

Smart Things to Know about **Customers**, ROS JAY

Smart Things to Know about **Decision Making**, KEN LANGDON

Smart Things to Know about **E-Commerce**, MIKE CUNNINGHAM

Smart Things to Know about **Innovation & Creativity**, DENNIS SHERWOOD

Smart Things to Know about **Knowledge Management**,
TOM M. KOULOPOULOS & CARL FRAPPAOLO

Smart Things to Know about **Managing Projects**, DONNA DEEPROSE

Smart Things to Know about **Marketing**, JOHN MARIOTTI

Smart Things to Know about **Partnerships**, JOHN MARIOTTI

Smart Things to Know about **People Management**, DAVID FIRTH

Smart Things to Know about **Strategy**, RICHARD KOCH

Smart Things to Know about **Teams**, ANNEMARIE CARACCIOLO

Smart Things to Know about **Your Career**, JOHN MIDDLETON

You can stay **Smart** by e-mailing us at **info@wiley-capstone.co.uk**
Let us keep you up to date with new Smart books, Smart updates, a Smart newsletter and Smart seminars and conferences. Get in touch to discuss your needs.

C A P S T O N E

Smart

THINGS TO KNOW ABOUT

E-Business

MIKE CUNNINGHAM

The right of Michael J. Cunningham to be identified as the author of this work has been asserted in accordance with the Copyright, Designs and Patents Act 1988

First published 2002 by
Capstone Publishing Limited (A Wiley Company)
8 Newtec Place
Magdalen Road
Oxford OX4 1RE
United Kingdom
http://www.capstoneideas.com

CIP catalogue records for this book are available from the British Library and the US Library of Congress

ISBN 1-84112-169-X

Typeset in 11/15pt Sabon by
Sparks Computer Solutions Ltd, Oxford, UK
http://www.sparks.co.uk

Substantial discounts on bulk quantities of Capstone books are available to corporations, professional associations and other organizations. Please contact John Wiley & Sons for more details on 212 850 6000 or (fax) 212 850 6088 or (e-mail) info@wiley-capstone.co.uk

Printed and bound by Antony Rowe Ltd, Eastbourne

To all of those souls lost on September 11, 2001,
and to the beloved that are rebuilding the lives that surrounded them

Contents

What is Smart?

The *Smart* series is a new way of learning. *Smart* books will improve your understanding and performance in some of the critical areas you face today like *customers, strategy, change, e-commerce, brands, influencing skills, knowledge management, finance, teamworking, and partnerships.*

Smart books summarize accumulated wisdom as well as providing original cutting-edge ideas and tools that will take you out of theory and into action.

The widely respected business guru Chris Argyris points out that even the most intelligent individuals can become ineffective in organizations. Why? Because we are so busy working that we fail to learn about ourselves. We stop reflecting on the changes around us. We get sucked into the patterns of behavior that have produced success for us in the past, not realizing that it may no longer be appropriate for us in the fast-approaching future.

There are three ways the *Smart* series helps prevent this happening to you:

- by increasing your self-awareness;

- by developing your understanding, attitude and behavior; and

- by giving you the tools to challenge the status quo that exists in your organization.

Smart people need smart organizations. You could spend a third of your career hopping around in search of the Holy Grail, or you could begin to create your own smart organization around you today.

Finally a reminder that books don't change the world, people do. And although the *Smart* series offers you the brightest wisdom from the best practitioners and thinkers, these books throw the responsibility on you to *apply* what you're learning in your work.

Because the truly smart person knows that reading a book is the start of the process and not the end ...

As Eric Hoffer says, "In times of change, learners inherit the world, while the learned remain beautifully equipped to deal with a world that no longer exists."

David Firth
Smartmaster

Preface

Since the publication of the first edition of this book, much has changed. The meltdown of many dotcoms has occurred. Many businesses have figured out how they can use Internet-based technologies to improve the way they operate. Industry and individuals have moved beyond whether to use the Internet. The Internet has landed and so has everyone else. We now know that we have to take notice, we cannot remain Luddites.

We are now reaching another phase in the development of the Internet and the World Wide Web that may be scarier than the first round. While many organizations have already moved into the sector, using technology as a weapon in their arsenal, the rules continue to change and impact our actions for the future. More so than ever, the way in which we embrace e-business technologies will affect our potential for success, or increase our opportunity to stumble.

In the first edition, I emphasized the need for organizations to consider how we deal with change, and e-business was the topic that was going to ensure that we did so. While much has changed in the technology and the marketplace since 1999, the requirement for change has not. It still drives our every need and movement in this segment.

As managers and professionals in organizations today we are faced with change as a normal way of life. We are in a world that expects us not only to know what is going to happen next, but to have predicted the solution so we are ready to exploit change when it comes. E-business tools can be a great catalyst to assist in the facilitation of this change, but we have to understand the fundamentals in order to take the appropriate action. The technology confusion is still with us. We still have as many definitions of the subject as there are vendors and suppliers in the marketplace.

This book sets out to provide guidance for you to navigate these waters. Over the course of the next eight chapters, you will start to understand the relationship between the complex elements of e-business and how they affect an organization and a marketplace.

E-business is not just about technology; it allows us to craft new ways of doing business differently. A fundamental goal of this book is to help you understand the relationship between the technology components and the other things that have to change in an organization in order to support it. For many years I have been a frustrated participant in the computing industry. Frustrated because the industry has made it so hard for others to make good decisions about technology and how to use it effectively. The industry has always focused on just one aspect of the problem. The vendors tout the technology and what it can do, consultants have espoused re-engineering while ignoring the technology components, as a result there are many confused technologists and managers out there.

The very high failure rates of most information technology projects continue to scare the best of us. According to more recent surveys, these are getting worse, not better. I believe that one reason that this rate is so high is related to the poor integration of business goals, work process change and technology in determining plans. We also have a tendency to acquire technology in the same way as we did in the 70s and 80s, using Request For Proposals and long buying cycles. By the time we reach a conclusion the technology has changed twice, and so may our business.

Smart Things To Know about E-Business takes aim at these problems. Firstly, you will be armed with the necessary information to understand where the "bodies are buried" before you start out on your journey. Understanding the technology, its impact on the organization, and the importance of new business models should help clear the way forward. You will not be an expert in any one of the areas covered within, but you will be smart. You will understand their importance and relevance to your own industry or organization segment. I also hope that you will be better able to determine which types of systems are most relevant to your needs.

As nothing helps us succeed like success, I have taken many examples, quotes and references from others who have been e-business pioneers and visionaries.

Building a guide for e-business strategies is rather like producing a history course at the same time that the war is raging in the field. Difficult, particularly when the battlefield and tactics are changing frequently. We learn on a day-to-day basis, and need to take what we have learned to battle the next day.

We have never been faced with tools and strategies that can give us direct access to so many consumers and customers or partners in record time. Likewise, your competitors have never had such easy, direct access to your client base. Electronic information on all of us is being bought and sold to a broad range of companies targeting our purses and wallets. Similarly, the trends occurring in the business-to-business (B2B) segment have already had a staggering impact on the marketplace.

Smart Things To Know about E-Business will help you understand where to look for new e-business strategies and solutions to address this complex new world facing us. We can ignore what is going on out there, or we can embrace it. Regardless of whether you decide to embrace or ignore, understanding how and why these systems are important could be one of the most important business issues you will ever face. Whether you are reading for the development of your career, improving your organization's operations, or are considering starting your own company, this book will help you define and refine your plans.

The strategies included in this book are based on practical experience and a successful record of accomplishment in developing, implementing and creating value for organizations using e-business systems. Every element of the book is touched by the tactical consulting programs and systems used at the Harvard Computing Group, Inc. I am deeply grateful to the staff there for their input in the development of this book.

This book will help you learn about e-business and the changes it brings. It will help you get ready for it, and tackle it more effectively. Adopt or become a victim. If you do not want to change, do not worry your competition will make you change, or face extinction. I say this not to scare you. It's just that a well-executed e-business program can create value and absorb market share at rates that we have never seen before. Used effectively, e-business has a much greater power than the number of people in the company. E-business can leverage intellectual property in a way we could not imagine a few years ago. This level of marketing capacity has previously been limited to the very largest corporations, those with the biggest brand

and budget capabilities. The targeting of individuals and their needs has been the bailiwick of niche markets and small players. The Internet and e-business can let a company have both.

I have spent most of my career focusing on the application of computing technology to solve practical business problems. Sometimes these have been about building new and complex software systems. In other cases I have helped organizations integrate their work process and technology solutions in a common framework. In all cases I have tried to link the technology to the business need. Without this primal connection, we have a tendency to produce useful weapons but ones focused on the wrong target. This book will help you improve your aim.

Smart quotes

"Now this is a knife."

Paul Hogan (Comparing his 6-inch bowie knife to the switchblade of his attacker in the movie *Crocodile Dundee*)

I have also continued to be surprised about the lack of tools out there to help the individual business owner, the rising middle manager, the executive, to understand how to apply technology to business problems. *Smart Things To Know about E-Business* will help you develop strategies and programs specifically for e-business problems.

What is all the fuss about?

Rarely has a subject been more touted than e-business in recent years. This is not surprising really, because e-business is all about money. Lots of money. While we have overcome the euphoria of the dotcom IPOs, the value that has been created by new players and existing firms leveraging the tools has been incredible.

Reason may have returned to the stock market, but the way that we do business will never be the same again. E-business is a way of improving the way an organization is working and is based on the following principles:

- collecting money from consumers;

- collecting money from business partners (supply chain);

- improving the productivity of current processes;

- developing and supporting new automated processes;

- changing how you deal with existing customers; and

- changing how you deal with new customers.

Almost all e-business strategies and programs can be attached to these principles. In fact, if you cannot connect them, then it is probably not e-business that you are looking at, but some other Internet-based scheme that is unlikely to be worth pursuing.

Smart Things To Know about E-Business is written for those individuals and managers who face these changes and challenges. It will help you become better armed to deal with them, and understand the important relationship between e-business and our organizations today, and in the future.

Although this is a very technical subject, the function of the components and how they work together is not so complex. *Smart Things To Know about E-Business* will not make you a technical expert, but you will have enough knowledge to identify the components and their relationship with the other important elements that make e-business systems work.

Smart Things To Know about E-Business is not intended to be a change-management handbook. Rather it will provide you with guidelines to help you find your own solutions.

My own experiences with e-business have taught me to continue to be inquisitive, open and receptive to new ideas. As a consultant in this industry, I am frequently asked to comment, revise or validate business ideas and strategies in this market. The creative mind of an entrepreneur with a new idea, why they dreamt it up in the first place and how they plan to bring it to market is often a joy to behold. There are many ways to build a business with e-business as the hub. Sometimes we need to consider some more radical ideas and business models to make it work. Other solutions demand large changes in how we work with our partners. Keeping an open mind is one of the greatest assets in the development of systems. Do not become locked in by one technology, a single strategy or the marketplace, as it might exist today. The days of the business model that can be predicted for five years without change are over, (aside from nationalized industries that control the marketplace and demand).

Another factor that really affects our thinking in e-business is *time*. Many successful managers assume that they have little time to get to market. They also assume that their enemy is working on the same thing and have twice as many resources applied to the problem.

We need to be ready for change in our thinking, our strategy and our business plans. An open mind and readiness for change may be the most important assets we can bring to the table in an e-business strategy. Knowing our market is a substantial third to these factors.

I hope that *Smart Things To Know about E-Business* will make you more aware of how technology components will influence your e-business strategies. You should be able to see more clearly how to build a plan for a system and see how your current business processes and a potential e-business solution can work together. I also hope that you will find the extensive quotations, references and examples of other systems useful for you in your quest. After all, we all need to see the tactics that the successful generals are using if we are to have a chance of winning our own battles.

Mike Cunningham
Grand Cayman Islands
July 16, 2001
email: mcunningham@harvardcomputing.com
telephone: 978 692 6766 x204 (office)
fax: 978 692 1864
mail: Harvard Computing Group, Inc.
238 Littleton Road,
Westford, MA 01451
USA

1

E-Business – The History of the Internet "So Far"

What the Internet is, and how to compare it with previously chronicled technology changes is not a simple task. The Internet provides us with a framework for business, yet we can also play games. We can shop and we can learn, find partners and do research, watch TV and gamble. Many of the things we do in our everyday life we can do on the Internet. The Internet has meant change for us, we have experienced the early years, but as James Champy quipped at a recent conference "We are ten minutes into a 24-hour poker game." We know that this means that we have already had to change, but still we are not sure how much more will come.

The overnight success that we know as the Internet actually celebrated its 32nd birthday in 2001. In terms of history however, we have to consider the Internet a youngster, a youth with an interesting heritage, one worth reviewing.

If you are familiar with the evolution of the Internet, or do not care how and why it came into being, please skip this chapter and go directly to Chapter 2.

The evolution of the Internet

Despite the fact that the Internet has been popular only in the past few years, it is difficult for us to imagine a world without its presence. The daily barrage of new sites, special deals, business offers and applications changes that meet us headlong are mind-boggling. We now consider the Internet part of our desktop for the most part and have to learn how to deal with it. We want our kids to use it for research, but are wary of the consequences of them traveling to unplanned or undesired destinations. The Internet has, it seems, become a center for commerce and global swindles in an instant of time.

The US Government started the process as they laid the framework for the Internet in the 1960s. A decision was made to fund a network of computers that would all talk the same language. This connected research, government workers and contractors (providing systems and data to the government agencies) using common protocols. As most computers at this time had very different communication systems to talk to each other (known as protocols), a new system was developed for this purpose. This network was known as ARPAnet, and incorporated the now very popular TCP/IP networking protocol. The standards in this protocol permitted reliable transmission of data from one computer to another, and the networked communications of data between each computer connected to the ARPAnet. This provided the foundation for the Internet as we know it today.

Another other major US government requirement was to ensure that the system was secure and would allow continued communication between

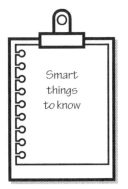

Smart
things
to know

REDUNDANCY

Instant fail-safe backup of computer systems to ensure that they continue to operate effectively in the case of a single or multiple point of failure

these sites and computers in the case of nuclear attack. Therefore, the serious requirement of redundancy of the Internet was built into the system from the word go.

> **KILLER APPLICATION**
>
> An incredibly useful, creative program that provides a breakthrough for its users. The first killer app of the Internet was email.

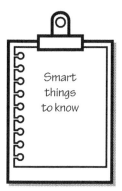

Smart things to know

As the Internet evolved from a military focus towards non-military use, the first killer application of the Internet was born: electronic mail. Despite the fact that the ARPAnet had been built for the transfer of data between computers, electronic communication became the first wave of adoption. The ability to communicate electronically using this medium was very popular. Over this same period, office productivity applications were developing, firms such as WANG were making millions from specialized computers providing office functions across a proprietary network. These networks were very useful for medium to large-scale organizations, but still not affordable by smaller businesses.

The role of the personal computer

Enter the personal computer: here was the device that was going to make a difference. Suddenly, the power of medium-size mini-computers had scaled to a new level. Early 1985 saw the first serious PC products to market and the adoption rate was phenomenal. In the United States this was further exaggerated by early adopters, who purchased computers partially as a statement of their liberation from internal IT purchasing policy. Departments could make decisions about computers without their being bogged down in months of bureaucratic effort involving the MIS department. In particular

Apple, developers of the Macintosh, drove a marketing program close to a religious frenzy. (Their recent revival is also based on a marketing strategy where their customers "think differently" from the masses.)

The PC started a revolution in the development (and the cost) of software products. No longer was software development something confined to the mid-range and high-end systems. The personal computer provided a new entry point for developers of software, and the leaders in the businesses understood this trend. Bill Gates left Harvard University early to take advantage of the market opportunity. (Did rather well didn't he?) Steve Jobs identified another killer application – desktop publishing for the Macintosh – and Adobe and many software vendors headed for the start-up capital and an expanding marketplace.

As all this was going on, the IT market became very polarized. Mid-range and high-range vendors tried to ignore the PC and allowed new vendors to build their businesses at an incredible rate. As IBM and Intel left the door open from the architecture perspective (although IBM tried later to close it with OS/2 and microchannel) the market grew. New companies such as Dell, Compaq and Gateway forged their way in the marketplace, building PCs from this open architecture. All of this provided the framework for the next market demand.

Organizations now had a collection of productive islands of computing, but needed to leverage them. The answer was to connect their machines to form a network. Banyan and Novell built entire companies around the network-

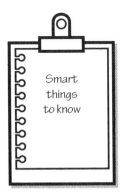

Smart
things
to know

LOCAL AREA NETWORK (LAN)

A computer network that operates and is located in one specific location. Many of these may be connected together in order to enable users to share resources and information on their network.

ing of PCs and other machines. The world of workgroup computing and the local area network was born. Initially the applications were simple. File sharing and printing provided the foundation of many of those early systems. However, with the entry level for software firms now lower than ever before, the opportunity to develop and distribute systems at a lower cost created hundreds of start-ups to write software for the PC.

The reason that this information is important to the evolution of the Internet is simple. The Internet is a network of computers, and it works in the same way as the local area network, with a few differences. It has an industry standard protocol for communication between systems, and a common language to converse and present data between differing systems.

Figure 1.1 illustrates how information networks are constructed. If an individual wants to communicate with these systems, they require access to this Private Data Network. These networks are the basis of many computer operations around the world. You need to understand the differences between

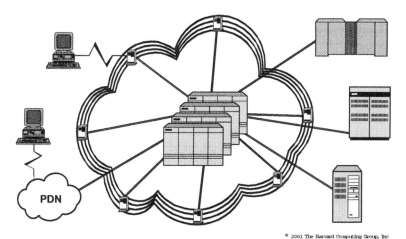

Fig. 1.1 Information networks.

the private networks and the public one we call the Internet (Table 1.1). Many large firms also manage their own private networks to meet their specific security and business requirements.

Table 1.1 Sample of differing services and their function.

Service	Private or public	Function
America Online	Private	Email access, information services, www access, shopping
MSN	Private	Email access, information services, www access, shopping
Internet	Public	Email access, www access

Of all networks, the Internet represents the largest collection of computers in the world today. The growth has been meteoric in recent years, but it took a while to get started. Figure 1.2 tells the story of adoption in recent years.

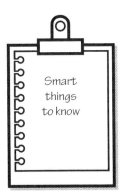

Smart things to know

DOMAIN NAME

The unique name that is used to identify a Web site. It contains two or more parts separated by a dot. Up until recently, domain names fitted into one of seven categories: educational institutions; commercial organizations; military; government; non-profit organizations; networking organizations; and international organizations (e.g. www.harvardcomputing.com).

The components of the Internet world

In order to understand just how open and powerful the Internet has become, we need to review a few more details of its components. Every computer on the Internet has its own unique name. This is called a domain name, in addition to the domain name, each system has an extension. The extension usually describes the general function of the holder of the domain name.

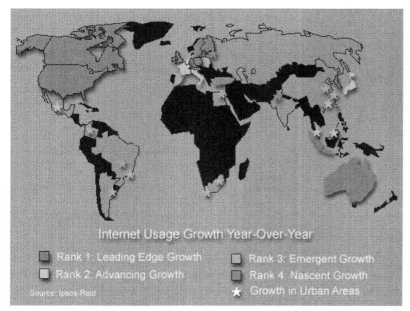

Internet Usage Growth Year-Over-Year

☐ Rank 1: Leading Edge Growth   ☐ Rank 3: Emergent Growth
☐ Rank 2: Advancing Growth   ☐ Rank 4: Nascent Growth
Source: Ipsos-Reid   ★ Growth in Urban Areas

Fig. 1.2 Internet usage and growth characteristics. Source: IPOS-Reid.

Although there have recently been some changes in the use of extensions, they generally adhere to the following principles. The .coms are usually companies or commercial operations, .nets are often Internet Service Providers, .mil is the military and so on.

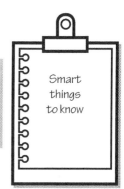

Smart
things
to know

ICANN (THE INTERNET CORPORATION FOR ASSIGNED NAMES AND NUMBERS)

Governing body controlling the issue and control of Internet domains and addresses.

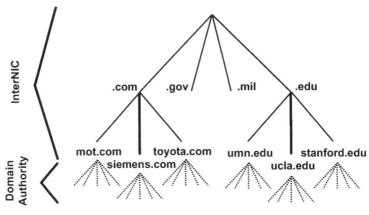

Fig. 1.3 Domain names and Internet organization.

More recently, country and other extensions are becoming sought after. The .cc, and .tv extensions are particularly popular. New company-based extensions are under consideration and being released. For computers to talk to one another on the Internet, a valid domain name is required to make the connection. Each of these unique connections allows us to ensure that we always connect to a valid member of the Internet, and that the members have become Internet citizens through a policing that used to be known as the Internic. This authority has been replaced by a governing and licensing body (Shared Registration System) that allows approved organizations to manage and issue domain names. This authority ensures that each name is unique and managed independently through this process. New mechanisms are now being set up as further extensions are being made to the domain name world, most recently the .biz and. .info extensions.

When we connect to the Internet, we connect to a network. In a typical workgroup organization this connection is usually a physical connection to a network in the office. We get around this problem with remote access by

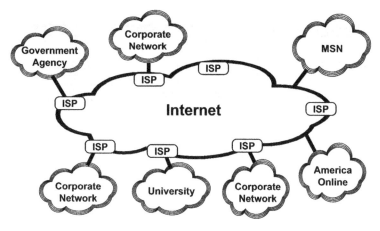

© 2001 The Harvard Computing Group, Inc

Fig. 1.4 Components making up the Internet and Internet-enabled networks.

using dial-up connections using a modem to connect to remote computers in the system. These computers then become part of the network.

There are many applications on the Internet, but the most common and frequently used ones are those in Table 1.2. Even if you are not familiar with some of these applications it is very likely that someone in your organization is using some or all of these applications in support of your Web site or internal applications. Over time, more and more of these applications are becoming available via a simple browser interface, avoiding the need for specialized software or interfaces.

Hosting and Internet Service Providers

Access to these applications and others are provided by companies with lots of computing resources, high-performance connections to the Internet and secure computing facilities known as data centers.

Table 1.2 List of major application products and tools for Internet-based applications.

Application	Function	Product used
Electronic Mail	Interpersonal and worldwide communication of electronic messages and files.	Any email enabled browser, or Internet compatible email client software
Browser applications for the WWW	Visit sites, or run Web-based applications.	Browser software from Microsoft, Netscape or other systems
Bulletin Board	Information transfer to specific databases that are by invitation only	Most bulletin boards are now accessible via Web browsers
FTP (File transfer protocol)	Provides a way to upload and download data and software to and from Web sites. Can be public or private access.	FTP transfer software programs.
Newsgroups	Provide discussion groups that are useful for industry and professional information. Information is shared.	Most browsers, support newsgroup functions directly
Chat and Instant messaging	Interactive (almost) discussion groups with members pre-selecting themselves	Instant messenger, Netscape AOL Microsoft instant messenger, ICQ, Service specific chat rooms.
Conferencing	Various means of communicating with others via the Internet, used for voice, video and data conferencing	Microsoft NetMeeting and many more on the market. Now often offered as part of a site service, with the hosting included.
Communications and search tools	Telnet allows you to log into remote computers, Gopher is now built into most browsers today.	Included with most browsers and transparent for users today.
Mail list servers	Designed to allow bulk email delivery to a selected group of individuals	Offered by most Internet Services Providers as option. Can be purchased as software products.
Video clips (streaming video)	Provides a method to deliver real time video to the desktop of the user (if the bandwidth and server systems are able to support the requirements for the systems)	Microsoft, Apple and Real Networks are the major players with tools and systems to deliver to the desktop.

These centers are often built to withstand significant natural weather disasters, have their own generators as back-up, and are often "duplicated" in a huge network to provide a fail-safe recovery means for data in the event of the power failure. The large ones such as America Online have huge membership (50 million as of July 2001). Suppliers known as Internet Service Providers (ISPs) deliver general Internet access. These groups supply electronic mail services, Web page hosting, FTP access and of course external access to the Internet. Most companies reaching a certain size will opt for an Internet Service Provider to support their Internet access for a variety of reasons:

- it's cheaper;

- they do not have to deal with security or firewall issues internally;

- limited system maintenance required;

- screens junk mail;

- provides a hosting service for domain names (specific to the company requirements);

- provides support for the companies Internet users;

- can host email services if so desired; and

- offers e-commerce services and storefronts on a turnkey basis.

Q: What is the difference between the Internet and the World Wide Web?

A: The Internet is a collection of computers physically connected by a huge network and common communication protocols. The World Wide Web is one of a number of applications running across the computers on the Internet.

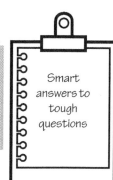

Smart answers to tough questions

As the Internet continues to expand the range of services offered in the marketplace, the range of companies and their activities is in constant flux. Despite these changes, there is still a continuous need to have access to the Internet. In the early stages, leading companies wanting to be on the Internet purchased bandwidth and Internet access from a telecom firm offering these services and then hosted their own system in-house with a dedicated communications link to the facility.

In early 1995, the market started to change. Many more firms and individuals wanted Internet access, but they either could not afford it or did not know how to do it themselves. (Setting up your own system in-house

Q: When should I consider a company-specific site, versus those provided by other services?

A: As soon as you have a need to "brand" your own organization or company site. This way you have you own identity and greater control over the content and the experience that your visitors will encounter.

requires significant knowledge on security and firewall systems to avoid external unauthorized access to internal computer systems.)

Consequently, two types of services emerged in the marketplace. Service providers primarily focused on the individual user, who needed to browse the Internet and have access to on-line information services, and a new breed of firms emerged known as Internet Service Providers. This second

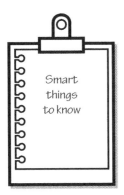

INTERNET SERVICE PROVIDER (ISP)

Internet Service Providers deliver a wide range of services to individual users and organizations for the Internet. These include Web hosting, electronic mail, FTP, and many other e-business services.

group focused on providing email, Web hosting, ftp and other services to small and medium size businesses. This allowed firms to establish a Web presence, have relatively high-speed access (better than dial-up services), but not have to install dedicated software and computer systems to host their Web sites, or manage their Internet email. Firms and services such as America Online, CompuServe, Prodigy, MSN grew quickly and a "marketing war" was declared for users and their service fees. Today there are still thousands of Internet Service Providers in the United States alone, despite more recent consolidation, and the market remains very competitive. However the range of services offered is changing, and changing fast.

One decision many of you will have to make early in your e-business strategy is how much of this is going to be brought in-house. In some cases, where security is critical, there are few choices. We do not expect banks or financial trading institutions to outsource the hosting of their systems anytime soon. However, many other businesses are outsourcing many of their important Internet-based information systems, and we expect this trend to continue.

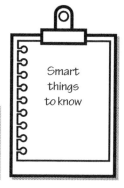

Smart things to know

APPLICATION SERVICE PROVIDERS

These are hosting services that will support, manage and maintain your mission-critical applications on their own computer systems.

In 1997 and 1998 another breed of firm entered the market. These dedicated high-end hosting providers offered some of the same services as the traditional ISPs, but with a twist. These firms focused on mission-critical applications that needed a lot of network bandwidth and reliability – the sort that could previously be obtained only by individual companies setting up their own data centers and back-up systems. Many applications such as voice and video needed huge network and computing resources. These firms became known as Application Service Providers. Now with a dramatically improved and mature technology infrastructure in place, many have become very successful.

This Application Service Provider segment is now quite mature. In these systems the service provider hosts the application on their computer systems, providing support and maintenance. In addition, some offer back-up and high-performance features such as mirroring, replication and access to on-demand bandwidth increases at peak times. Some of the application service providers also offer e-business features as part of hosting offerings for companies of all sizes.

The serious user will often opt to use a dedicated hosting provider. These companies provide the facilities that an organization might have to build for itself, (such as the data center), but share these facilities along with support for the applications that the company wants them to host. Many companies like this option, as it can save upfront costs for the Internet connection and can reduce maintenance costs over the life of the system. Companies such as Exodus and NaviSite have become fast-growing specialists in this sector of the market. More recently, large ISPs have started to acquire the ASP and hosting services to extend their offerings, creating global networks with service to support clients in many locations. UUNet is one such example, having acquired Digex in 2001 to provide this facility.

Intranets, and extranets

The tools of the Internet are not just for external use. It is relatively easy to take the architecture of the "big" Internet and scale it to use in your own environments. The following list of items will allow you to create your own "internal Internet:"

- a TCIP/IP network;

- electronic mail;

- Web server;

- a browser or client software application;

- chat; and

- FTP.

We now have the essential shopping list of what you need for an intranet. An intranet is your own organization's Internet. Here you have all the advantages of the Internet but customized to your own internal requirements.

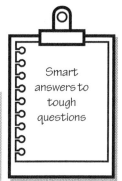

Smart answers to tough questions

Q: What is an intranet?

A: An intranet is an Internet network that is internal to the organization, and not generally accessible by the general public. It is based on the same technology components as the Internet.

Intranets have advantages over forms of groupware and office communication systems that they co-exist with. For example, they are:

- browser-based (everyone can be a user);

- people-friendly;

- easier to develop (than previous generation systems);

- easy to change;

- lower cost than traditional development alternatives;

- very high payback;

- based on standards that everyone should support;

- easier to update;

- easily customized;

- perform well; and

- scale better than most applications.

The development of an intranet has become a major component of many organizations' e-business strategy. Intranet systems evolve from many starting points. These run the gamut from strategic initiatives with enterprise support, to others developed at the departmental level and some that have been opportunistic, based on speed and cost constraints. Whatever the reasons, intranets have established themselves at the core of many IT strategies. Even organizations that have resisted the *gravitational pull* of the technology are adopting intranet strategies.

In the beginning, intranets were either located in data centers or out in the departments. In recent years, intranets within organizations are very common and have grown dramatically. This has created a need to integrate content, maintain performance, share information, control access and deal with intranets in differing locations. Multiple intranet servers, connected by local and wide area networks, provide the foundation for distributed intranets. Much of these systems are now linked into a portal strategy for the organization.

Today, most organizations have moved from the view that intranets are a separate component of their IT strategy. Intranets are a flexible way of organizing information where the content can be shared with others in a controlled and expandable way. This philosophy provides the foundation for the development of Distributed intranets. Also as intranets become richer in content, and this content is extended to partners and customers, more extranets are born. From the architectural point of view, the extranet is merely a protected section of the intranet (Fig. 1.5).

Web Browsing

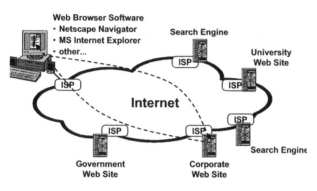

© 2001 The Harvard Computing Group, Inc

Fig. 1.5 The extranet.

Many firms develop intranets to improve productivity and increase the speed with which information is delivered inside their organizations. In environments that have a great need to provide accurate information in more timely and distributed ways, the intranet, with its natural ability to expand, has made it the technology choice of many. Intranets often provide the basis for the delivery of information that is needed by internal staff.

Table 1.3 Intranet applications and access characteristics.

Application	Intranet	Extranet
Employee telephone directory	Yes	Selected contact listing
HR policies	Yes	No
Support information	Yes	Yes, but controlled access
Knowledge base	Yes	Selected components on password protected basis

This evolution is not limited to *pure* intranet solutions, it also includes groupware, office and workgroup applications that either have or will become, Internet-based. Microsoft's .net strategy is a typical example of this move. These solutions are becoming more intranet-based, with browser-based interfaces, compatible with Web servers and supportive of Web standards. However, the underlying databases and data structures vary according to application and platform focus.

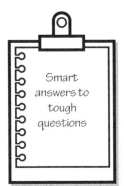

Smart answers to tough questions

> Q: What are the differences between an intranet and an extranet?
>
> A: Intranets are available only for internal staff; extranets are sections of generally proprietary information that organizations want to share with selected users on a controlled basis. They can be stand-alone, or a selected part of an intranet.

The extranet therefore becomes an external part of your Internet strategy, the part of your system that you want to communicate with your business partners and clients. Smart companies can achieve dramatic reduction of timeframes and costs with a careful combination of Internet, intranet and extranet programs. We will cover later the ingredients that you need to make all this work.

How Web software works

Internet-based software works by connecting with the target Web site and application that is driving the system. Unlike most other software applications we usually need only a browser to access and use most external Internet sites (Fig. 1.6). Software that is more complex is needed for security-controlled applications that we will look at later.

Once the request is made to the site, the Web server (along with supporting software systems) provides the results to the desktop of the requesting user.

Web Browsing

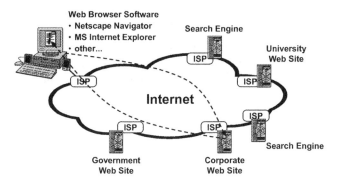

Fig. 1.6 How Internet software works.

TIM BERNERS-LEE

While working in Geneva, Switzerland at CERN, the European Particle Physics Laboratory, Berners-Lee created the World Wide Web. He is known as the father of the Internet.

SMART PEOPLE
TO HAVE ON
YOUR SIDE

Most of this conversation uses a language known as HTML (Hypertext Markup Language). Before the Internet, the idea of public access to so many software systems and computers with a single piece of software would have been considered unbelievable. The browser has changed our lives.

Software firms provide the ingredients for us to develop Internets, intranets and extranets. In the development of Internet technology, you will hear much about differing types of architecture, and how one is superior to the other. In general, there are two types of software firms in the market, ones that have developed their software specifically for the Internet and others that are changing their software to catch up with the others. Do not worry about any other software firms for your e-business strategy. You only want to do business with companies who recognize that the Web is where you want to be.

Software categorization for the Web can be very confusing for both the novice and the expert. Much of this is caused by a very fast-moving marketplace, and considerable vapor flying around in the marketing materials. (Later in the book, we will spend more time on the subject of selecting software vendors and partners.)

Technology food groups

The basic food groups that will influence our technology decisions on the Web are categorized below.

1   Horizontal applications

Most of the earlier applications and tools mentioned fit into this group. Electronic mail, newsgroups, bulletin boards, all fit these groups' requirements. Today, most of these have reached a commodity pricing level, and are included in other applications for a small fee. Until recently many of

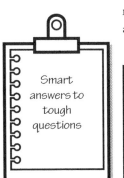

Smart
answers to
tough
questions

Q: What is a horizontal application?

A: Applications such as electronic mail, bulletin boards and chat systems are horizontal applications. These are ready to run, without much need for customization and can be used for many different internal or business-to-business (B2B) communication needs. They can be used to support many vertical or industry-specific functions.

these services were offered free, however things are changing, and most are now fee bearing applications.

2   Packaged applications

Turnkey applications that perform a particular application without major modification are becoming available for the Internet. Customer Management applications, Document Management systems and Project Management systems all fall into this category. Many of these were initially developed for client/server applications for local or wide area networks.

3   Web servers

The Web server is at the heart of any Web-based application. This is where data is stored, requested, and delivered to the appropriate applications, (these are usually browser based).

4   Database systems and application servers

Database products provide the information to be sent to Web servers and provide the transactions on the system. They are the brains of the system, where the most valuable information, trades and transactions are taking place.

5   Security systems

The most important aspect of your e-business solution. Without security you do not have a system, you have a liability. Security, typically, is defined at the computer, network, users, applications and even down to specific transactions.

6 Tools and other systems

A myriad of other tools are involved in the development of these systems, these include authoring, maintenance, administration, optimization, marketing and others. We will discuss these areas in more detail in Chapter 2.

7 Portals

Another type of site that is important to many operations today is the portal. The portal used to be viewed as a destination site for users of a particular class. However, today many organizations refer to their own environments as Corporate Portals, (primarily for B2B and B2E applications), and operations that consider their marketplace portals. (Vertical ones are sometimes referred to as vortals.)

Lines become blurred between dedicated portals and personalized e-business portals. The large portals that have evolved primarily from the search engines in the marketplace, now play a much bigger role. Incorporating shopping, research, communities, chat and email services, the battle for consumer-based mindshare goes on. Despite the success of the biggest ones, such as AOL, Yahoo!, Excite, and Lycos, searching for relevant information still remains a problem on the Internet that has yet to be solved.

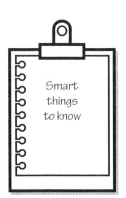

Smart
things
to know

PORTAL

Major visiting center for Internet users. The very large portals started life as search engines, AltaVista, AOL, Excite, Lycos, and Yahoo! are examples of major portals.

The portal market has changed. As Web users became smarter, they migrated to sites that offered them a more complete and relevant experience. In the business world, we have seen the birth of another form of portal, the Corporate Information Portal. This allows users to interact with information and systems relevant to the corporate world, and is customizable to meet their needs.

At the application end of the business, new portals are being defined, based on the use of a "free" service on the Web, such as email or calendaring. These features are now common on large portals such as Yahoo! and Lycos. (However, the *free* may be going out of some of these services before too long.)

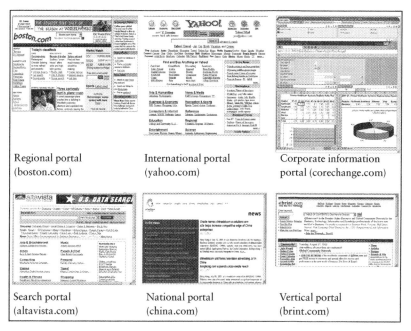

Regional portal
(boston.com)

International portal
(yahoo.com)

Corporate information
portal (corechange.com)

Search portal
(altavista.com)

National portal
(china.com)

Vertical portal
(brint.com)

Fig. 1.7 Examples of portals currently offering a mixture of services to visitors.

There is no question that the portal marketplace and what it means to us continues to change. As more companies with a presence on the Internet understand that content is one of the most important issues that continues to bring visitors back to their site, content-rich sites will continue to thrive. The vertical portal, focused on industry groups, has been one of the fastest-growing sections of the marketplace. If you want to stay abreast of activities in your industry, watch this space carefully. The vertical portals are going to ultimately change the way that business is done, particularly for partnership creation and business networking (Fig. 1.8).

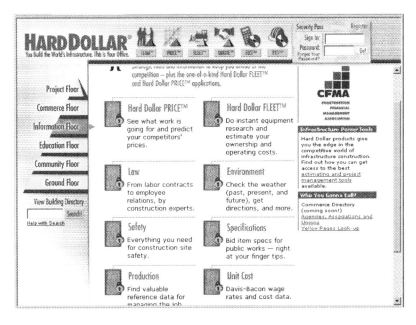

Fig. 1.8 Example of B2B portal in the construction industry (Hard Dollar Corporation).

8   Integrators and strategy development partners

Unless you have unlimited resources in your organization, it is likely that you will have to consider using some form of external help to deploy your system.

For most Web-based applications, companies and organizations will interact with systems integrators providing development resources. Many integrators offer packages in specific market and application areas.

Selecting integrators and development partners will be another important decision that you make with your e-business strategy. The wrong one will cause you many problems, the right one could be a reason for the dramatic expansion and success in your operation.

Determining what resources you need to help with the development will be based on areas in which you need assistance. Depending on your access to qualified internal resources, the balance of internal and external resources can vary. Some areas to consider for help include:

- strategy development;

- market research;

- application specification and project management;

- development and coding;

- quality assurance and testing; and

- roll-out and training.

Many consulting firms and vendors are now offering full service operations to assist businesses of varying sizes get rolling with their e-business systems. Today, most of them will start to drop the e- prefix from the offering, and are likely to envelope their offerings in an application-specific package.

When selecting partners in this process, understanding how you are going to use them is paramount in making good decisions. As many firms have been active in the e-business arena, there has been a severe shortage of developers and project managers with the right experience. However, it is less than ideal that you become the learning curve for developers or firms that do not have a track record of developing e-business systems. At the end of the day, you hire consultants to reduce risk and improve the potential for good outcomes of the project: this is not a time to pick the wrong firm.

Integration firms fall into several categories for e-business development, each having benefits, strengths and weaknesses for different types of work. Table 1.5 provides some guidelines of help for different types of assistance, with examples of firms in each category.

As you embark on the e-business road, consider the various elements and waypoints for your journey. There are many variables in this marketplace, and a continuously changing landscape. The trip will be exciting.

Picking partners is however, only one part of the process. First, we need to take a deep breadth and ready ourselves for the largest challenge of all: change.

Table 1.5 Types of development and consulting companies in the e-business market.

Project needs	Type of consulting firms	What to look for
Strategy consulting	E-business strategy development firms, management consulting firms specializing in e-business area	Track record of development of strategy through to the implementation of systems and company roll out
Research for e-business marketplace	Research firms specializing in e-business applications and markets	Specialized research capabilities to ensure that your target market is being addressed. Target marketing with good results for their client base
Application specification and project management	E-business strategy development firms, management consulting firms specializing in e-business area	Good project management skills, excellent facilitation and new work process skills. Most e-business systems require great change to occur in work process and practices
Development and coding, Quality Assurance and testing, Roll-out and training	Development firms specializing in e-business marketplace.	Strong development skills in e-business technology in your industry or technology area. High quality resources with good skills in high demand new relevant skills. References

2

Think E-Business – Think Change!

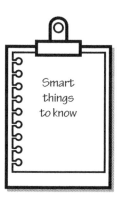

Smart
things
to know

Think e-business, think change. Probably the greatest factor driving most e-business strategies is the need for change and how best to leverage it. We are all facing change in our operations on a daily basis; e-business tools, used effectively, can help you make these changes occur rapidly. Considering the variables that you can work with to improve your operation is critical to understand how to make change happen. Leading companies have created dramatic value with their e-business initiatives and will continue to be successful. You can consider e-business tools as a weapon to change:

- strategy;

- technology;

- systems;

- separate business;

- sales activities and approaches;

- partnership strategies; or

- some combination of the above.

Many organizations look at e-business tools to improve one particular aspect of their business. For example, employee internal systems, or development of B2B supply chain systems. Most of the media spotlight on e-business has kept us focused on the business-to-consumer marketplace, buying products via the Web. This has in fact obscured our attention of what has been the larger part of this evolving marketplace, business-to-business e-business solutions.

The reasons for change

The business climate that has been affecting our ability to create and control change in our environments has itself been changing. These changes can be grouped into several categories and include:

- failure of new systems;

- fast changing markets and competitive environments; and

- the merging of collaborative and transaction-based e-business.

Failure of systems has rapidly become a leading cause of strategy and system change. Sometimes the failure has been technology implementation, but is not limited to this factor.

The continued very high failure rates of IT-related projects dog many operations, and e-business projects have been no exception. A recent survey conducted in the US indicated a continuing failure rate associated with these systems, and a particularly unnerving rate of more than 60% for systems including CRM technologies. While this small sample from the Gartner study may belie the success rates of others, it certainly delivers a "wake up call" for any embarking on IT projects of all sizes.

In addition to high failure rates, causing rework and rethinking of many systems and strategies, market changes contribute heavily to the need for change. Competitors that are also using e-business technology and systems

Average IT project statistics

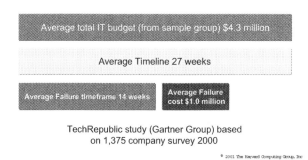

Average total IT budget (from sample group) $4.3 million

Average Timeline 27 weeks

Average Failure timeframe 14 weeks

Average Failure cost $1.0 million

TechRepublic study (Gartner Group) based
on 1,375 company survey 2000

© 2001 The Harvard Computing Group, Inc

Fig. 2.1 Industry continues to fail consistently to develop IT projects.

Up to 60% of projects to install CRM systems fail!

Source: Gartner Group

effectively can significantly affect the performance of any organization. Becoming ready to understand and meet these challenges often creates pressure for change in the organization.

Another factor now affecting many firms' e-business decisions is the merging of the collaborative and transactional elements of e-business systems. Increasingly, organizations are finding that unless the collaborative systems are in place, then many potential clients and partners cannot make transactional decisions on the Web site. This has caused many organizations to look to the simultaneous development of both collaborative and transactional e-business systems. Examples of these include:

- detailed product comparison information;

- product support information;

- configuration management systems; and

- access to inventory management tools and systems.

Preparing for change

In order to prepare ourselves for this type of change, we have to be ready to modify our behavior in a big way. Organizations prepare themselves to make these changes in several ways.

Staying current with technology and how it is being applied to your industry is a good starting place. However, this is only part of the process. You will also have to consider how you are going to determine what level of change is acceptable and the amount of risk that the organization is willing to take.

As e-business tools provide a competitive weapon, understanding the competitive pressures and trends is important in determining your strategy. Examining what your competitors are doing, and what is going in adjacent markets can deliver outstanding insights. While no one can force themselves to change, reading the "tealeaves" can provide good insight that will turn into action. Making changes too late could be harmful to the health of the business.

> Q: How do I evaluate risk in determining my e-business strategy?
>
> A: Imagine that you are working for your most feared competitor, that they have twice as much money to spend and can implement your e-business strategy in six months. Then decide how much risk is reasonable.

Smart answers to tough questions

In e-business, doing nothing has outcomes just like any other strategy or technology. If the market is in the early stages, it is possible that doing nothing can avoid wasted resources and finances. However, the leader who did it anyway may have failed, but they have also learned something in the process. Also, they are likely to have gained some specific skills in marketing, technology, support and organization change that will make it easier next time. Therefore, sometimes failing can cause you to win in the end. It is amazing how many firms have failed on the first and even second attempt at implementing e-commerce solutions. However, they keep coming back, they know that in the end this is a key factor for the success of their business.

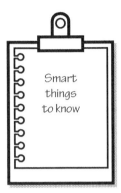

MOORE'S LAW

Intel founder Gordon Moore predicted that the performance (and chip density) of computers would double every 18 months while the price remains the same.

Smart people know how important the right mindset is to prepare for these changes. One of the best methods to weigh risk and reward is to look at how others have dealt with change.

The technology influence

Even if you decide to do nothing, the environment out there is going to change anyway. Your competitors and the marketplace continue to be affected greatly by the influence of technology.

Q: What two technological factors impact the adoption of e-business systems?

A: The systems are becoming more and more affordable, and the user base of customers is increasing dramatically over time.

Two technology laws are often quoted in the media that explain these factors. These are Moore's Law and, more recently, Metcalf's Law.

Moore's Law has a 32-year record of success since he predicted that computing technology would become increasingly affordable. However, it is Metcalf's Law, the law of connected computing that influences the

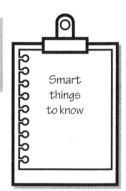
METCALF'S LAW

Robert Metcalf, founder of 3COM, predicted that the value of the network dramatically increases as every new node is added to the network

e-business space for all of us. The combination of these has produced a distributed computing world of customers with browsers at the ready.

We now have a market of millions of connected individuals, all linked to the same channel. In the last few years we have started to exploit the benefits of collaboration.

Although technology never makes a marketplace on its own, it has provided the vehicle. Internet technology is available everywhere on the planet, allowing products and services to be offered on a scale never possible before. Just consider how research was done before the Internet. Some schools in the United States will currently not let kids submit their research based on what they have found out on the Internet. Why? Because they want kids to learn how to do traditional research, to understand how to use a library and other published materials to come to conclusions. We have come to expect instant results and conclusions.

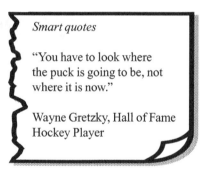

Smart quotes

"You have to look where the puck is going to be, not where it is now."

Wayne Gretzky, Hall of Fame Hockey Player

With such a large amount of data available, finding the relevant information can be the challenge for most of us. But wait for it, there are products coming onto the market specifically to address this issue.

The market consolidates ...

As the Internet has developed, we have moved through several evolving business models. The only guarantee that we have seen in the marketplace is continuous change. This changing landscape is what we can expect for our future.

One aspect of this is what was free and what we pay for on the Internet. Table 2.1 illustrates how businesses are offering services for increasingly powerful and complex applications, but now firms are changing their strategies and starting to charge for these services.

Table 2.1 Examples of how Internet costs have changed, and continue to change.

Service	Initially	Currently (2001)	In the future
Searching (via public portals)	Free	Free	Free
Electronic mail	Subscription	Subscription and Free	Subscription and free
Bulletin boards	Subscription	Subscription and Free	Subscription
Newsgroups	Free	Free	Free
Instant messaging	Subscription	Subscription and Free	Free
Individual hosting services	Subscription	Subscription and Free	Subscription
Extranet services	Software based fee	Subscription and software fee	Free, subscription and software fee
Mail list servers	Software based fee, subscription service	Subscription service (some software products)	Subscription
Web hosting	Subscription based	Subscription and free	Subscription and free

As we move from the early euphoric days of *free* everything, business models that give away services and products do so only when it supports their business models. Do not be fooled by this. Many of the sites and companies putting money into subsidizing these services are doing it for several good reasons.

Smart things to say

Aside from the last reason, there is method in the madness of giving things away on the Internet. While there has been a considerable "tail off" in the delivery of free services to clients, as many business models never "made it" to the money-making stage, there are still good reasons to provide "free services" and "information" to target clients. Keeping groups of existing or prospective customers in communities of interest is without doubt one of the most cost effective forms of electronic marketing.

Most operations that have made good use of these services have now become reliant on the free services, to the point that their e-business systems would not work without them. For example, mail list services, several of which were free until recently, have now become a paid-for service. As investors move towards more rapid payback timeframes for Internet-based services, costs to users will increase and consolidation of suppliers and operators will increase.

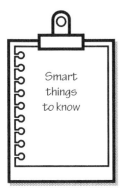

BROCHUREWARE

The act of putting your corporate literature in basic static form directly to a Web site. Often bores visitors to death, and causes rapid exits from the site.

Traditional entry to the market could be harmful to your health.

So smart people know that considering only traditional approaches could be the very thing that causes an e-business strategy to fail before you have even started.

In the early stages of many companies' strategies on the Web, there is a rush to put up what was called a "vanity site" or "brochureware." Amazingly, since the first edition of this book, there are many substantial companies who still have sites that reflect this approach. The sites are static and not well maintained. Many even have spelling mistakes and old addressees and inconsistent information. For any company wanting to present a reasonable image to their clients, this is the equivalent of unpleasant graffiti all over the walls of your headquarters. Unacceptable.

Leave tradition for weddings and funerals. It will not do you any good on the Web, aside from leveraging your brand. Understanding how to develop innovative approaches without great risk is the mark of many successes in this industry. But don't expect it to be cheap. Despite what you may have heard, building (and promoting) a good Web site is not cheap. I do not care how good your 13-year-old kid is with the latest Web tool, they will not be able to represent your corporation as well as a firm that knows how to translate your goals into a finished system. You may get what you paid for, a cheap job.

Most companies and organizations have now to consider their objectives for their site before they get started. Don't just replicate the corporate literature and expect it to be a winner.

Change thinking

Identification of the important objectives for your e-business site is your most important starting point. Use these goals as the vehicle for setting about your change in approach in the marketplace. Some sample questions to consider are:

Q: What are the smart questions to ask before starting an e-business development?

A: • What type of visitors do you want to visit your site?
   • How many of them do you need to market effectively?
   • What message do you want them to get?
   • Do you want to build a community?
   • Is the site a transaction site?
   • Are there customer support requirements?

Acclimatizing yourself and others in the organization to this type of thinking is a good warm-up to the real development of the strategy.

Smart answers to tough questions

We need to:

• provide on-line customer support function;
• sell products on-line; and
• create community of interested prospects.

Smart things to say

Table 2.2 Sample business goals and e-business goals.

Business goals	e-business goals
Provide on-line customer support function	Create a self-service customer support database that will fulfill 60% of current help desk calls
Sell products on-line	Build secure e-business facility for existing and new clients
Create community of interested prospects	Develop "vertical interest" to provide visitors with a reason to visit and return.

A process of new strategy development needs a different mindset to consider how to develop and implement the system. If you create a clear set of business goals and then transfer them to objectives for the e-business strategy, you will reduce risk from the business strategy. E-business goals should be a pure reflection of any overall objectives for your audience.

Competition, it may be closer than you think

We often consider competition as one of the final reasons for change and e-business (unless you have left it really late in your market space). Competitors can use the Internet as an unfair advantage, and in fact this is a smart way to look at developing e-business systems. Leveraging what you already have in place will make a dramatic difference to how you bring your strategy into play.

For example, consider two medium-size furniture companies that are both looking to put e-business systems in place for their distributors.

Company A decides to take an aggressive approach, knowing that Company B does not have a serious Web presence. They want to get there first.

Company A decides to take a "get their fast" approach and hires a local Web designer to come "get them up and running in 30 days or less"

The process looks like this:

- web designer A reviews Company A's brochures and company;

- provides a boiler plate site framework, with the usual About Us, Message from the President, Mission and a nice walk through of their furniture line with descriptions and sample pictures; and

- Company A approves the new site.

They are up and running on the Web in advance of their competition. Goal achieved.

When developing your strategy, look at high value and high impact changes that will generate big returns for you, your clients and shareholders.

Smart things to say

Company B takes a different approach. Company B looks at their overall business goals. These include reducing inventory turns, increasing sales, and gaining better performance from its distribution network.

Company B conducts some internal review of these goals and determines that there are some serious problems with their distribution channel and loyalty with their dealers. Then they hire a consultant to determine the business and technical requirements of their new system.

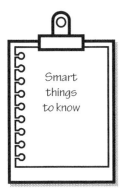

Smart
things
to know

PLANNING TO WIN

- Understand the market conditions;
- review the space for your competitors;
- analyze how e-business-focused you already are;
- review your competitiveness; and
- decide how fast your segment will adopt e-business systems.

This process produces a realization that:

- More loyalty and customer satisfaction could be achieved by allowing business partners to place orders and get delivery dates for orders via a controlled extranet application.

- By designing an e-business system to integrate with existing manufacturing and inventory management system, its partners can gain access to this information easily.

- Because of this service, customers visiting their distributors' stores are offered almost instant information about delivery schedules. (Company A clients will have to wait till the store is open on Monday, and get a telephone call response, well after their client has left the store while shopping at the weekend.)

- It can develop a Web site that has a theme for different types of decorating tastes and styles and it can organize the site so clients can view the furniture by manufacturer, style or taste.

- A search capability could be added to the site to let distributors and their customers find furniture based on style.

Although Company B came to market later with their solution, the results they achieved were much more significant. They thought through how they were going to use the technology to help achieve their business goals. (A surprising number of firms still do the technology first, and then hope it will do something for the business.) They also used a firm that could translate their business goals into a system that would give them a sustainable competitive advantage over their competitors. The other firm's clients still have to make a telephone call before they can determine availability of the product their client needs.

> Leverage your existing technology and systems to improve customer service and support improved sales cycles.

Smart things to say

Second-guessing your competitors

Another good strategy to use in warming up for e-business change is to play out the following scenario.

1   You define your new product strategy for e-business.

2   Next you launch the product.

3   Then your competition comes out with a revised or more competitive offering to your new product.

4   What do you do?

The answer is of course to consider the reaction (#4) before you launch the product. This way you will examine how others may counter your strategy before it comes to market, therefore allowing you to review either the existing plan, or be ready with some alternative changes as they come to the marketplace. Many firms do not consider this scenario in the marketplace, and then are sideswiped by the competition. Despite what we might think personally, we often do not have a monopoly on the same idea or strategy.

Traditional marketing strategies don't always work

In the world of traditional markets we have a set of reference points that do not always do us favors. Many software (and other) companies that are focusing on the Internet exclusively have developed their strategies by being very contrary to conventional business thinking. Some of the leading firms on the Internet today were started on a shoestring. They all had in common that they wanted to create a "community" of users, and provide a valuable experience at their sites (e.g. Yahoo!). Others have spent vast amounts of money to create huge user communities or to develop a "brand" at any cost (e.g. Amazon.com, America Online).

Traditional marketing strategies can cause the effect outlined in Table 2.3.

Table 2.3 Traditional strategies can enforce limited results.

Traditional strategy	Potential outcome
Stick to existing business model and try and replicate it on the Web	Does not provide significant improvement in sales, service or customer satisfaction
I will sell my existing product on the Web	May be more opportunities to offer broader range of product on or via the Web
Protect my existing distribution strategy	Some of the current distribution channels may not be adding enough value to warrant protection. May leave money on the table
Limit impact on internal operations	Minimizes the opportunity for productivity improvements

"Out of the box thinking" is often referred to as a method of ensuring that you do not limit the potential alternatives for your e-business system. That does not mean that you have to undertake seek-and-destroy missions throughout the organization, causing chaos and consternation everywhere. Nevertheless, smart people know that existing processes and situations can be improved dramatically.

To avoid some of these problems, and start the juices going just consider the way that traditional decision-making can result in the wrong type of change happening in the organization.

Avoiding bad decisions

As we outlined earlier in this chapter, the failure rates of IT systems continues to plague most of industry. While there are many benefits of scalability, reliability and connectivity associated with Internet-based systems, they also fail.

- 40% of IT projects were late or over budget;
- nearly 30% were abandoned, scaled back or modified; and
- only about 25% were completed on time and on budget.

Smart things to say about IT projects

Amazingly, we do not appear to be learning from our mistakes in technology selection, although the systems, software and implementation methodologies are more mature than ever before. Consolidation in industry, richer application development platforms and rapid application development tools should all lead us to greater implementation success. Why are failure rates so high? Here are some of the reasons why things go wrong.

Scenario one – The candy store

Many technology buys are just this, technology purchases. Users and management behave like kids in the veritable candy store. Thousands of dollars are spent buying generic research and visiting trade shows in an effort to become an expert on what is available in the marketplace. Don't make the mistake of spending too little time understanding how it will affect your business.

Scenario two – The crusade syndrome

Once enamored with a technology, there is usually no stopping the crusader. The battle cry becomes, "Now that I understand what's out there and know that I need one, all I have to do is convince all the others why they should have one too." Unfortunately, the outcome is often all too similar to the original crusades – lots of bloodshed and not as many converts as you would like.

Scenario three – Death by analysis

Analyze the problem to death and then specify the system needs. You cannot be wrong. Every possible requirement has been identified through a series of very expensive interviews and collated using a database or methodology ideally suited to the process. Every need has been homogenized, pasteurized, analyzed, qualified and prioritized. Now we have the "corporate view" encapsulated in a statistical representation of the whole organization's needs, but we have so much detail that nothing is clear. The technology has also probably changed while all this was going on.

Scenario four – Do it now, and do it fast!

Often following one of the above, particularly when it has taken too long, management issues an edict. The team is forced into action. Without a game plan, they are forced to react. Emergency decisions produce emergency results, which are seldom satisfactory.

We get what we deserve

Buying technology without understanding our business goals and how we are going to use it is a recipe for failure. (Who has not been responsible for a "shelfware" decision in their organization at some time?) If you buy a product and merely hope that people will use it, you will not succeed. Chapter 6 will deal with specific strategies to avoid any of the above problems.

Factor in the culture element

Another factor that influences our ability to change things in the organization is the cultural element. Creating the right environment for the adoption of the e-business system, and rewarding staff accordingly can make the difference between success and failure. Many organizations assume that traditional individual reward schemes will provide the incentive for change, but there are other issues that can cause the culture to reject the system.

Failure to understand and address these issues will ultimately influence the organization's achievements. Because so much of e-business productivity

Smart
things
to know about
culture issues

Table 2.4 Culture and work practice issues that affects deployment and success of e-business systems.

Example of culture	Result
Tremendous reward to individual efforts	More resistance to teambuilding and team rewarding initiatives
Entrapped in current work practices	Resistance to change
Hierarchical management	Difficult to adjust to collaborative team model
Driven by common corporate and employee goals/rewards	Rapidly adopt technology to support business and workgroup functions
Technology driven	Needs help to assist with workgroup productivity and process issues
Technophobic	Needs significant persuasion to use technology at all

gains are based on effective behavior change in the enterprise, it is critical to ensure that process change along with organizational culture modification is linked to the system. Understanding these issues will provide a dramatically increased potential for the success of the system.

Identifying candidates for change

Table 2.5 illustrates the importance of the relationships between the technology selection and the work practices inside the organization. Smart people will consider these relationships in your search for e-business candidate applications. As the technology has the ability to easily be driven to every desktop in the enterprise, consider the impact as information is distributed directly to the staff that need it. Even this simple change in the publishing and availability of information can cause consternation in an operation that has been used to a hierarchical management structure, with "trickle down" information flows.

Table 2.5 Examples of e-business technology influence inside the organization.

| Technology | | Work Process and practices | |
Before	After	Before	After
Departmental	Enterprise	Hierarchical	Across enterprise
Electronic publishing	Web publishing	Structured around release dates	Dynamic around change and organization needs
Application specific	Business function or organization specific	Information not easily re-purposed	Information re-purposed based on business needs
Client/server	Thin client	Not easily accessible from any point in organization	Easily accessible from any point in organization

Starting out to look for potential candidates for change is not as hard as you might think. Every business or organization has some areas that need improvement. Here are a few starting points to consider for e-business change.

You need to think about all of these:

- sales distribution strategies and support;
- improvements in customer support systems;
- changes in the distribution system;
- creating new products and services; and
- sales and distribution changes.

Smart things to say about e-business change

Industry trends and innovations

Industries are changing the way that they are using e-business as a lever. By focusing on the fundamental opportunities reviewed earlier great changes can and are being made. While we are still at an early stage of market development of these systems, pointers are starting to emerge for each market sector. There is barely an industry today that has been untouched by the e-business bug. Comprehending how this change will affect your operation may be reflected in what others are already doing. We all have to determine how and where best to effect this change.

Manufacturing and electronics

Manufacturing industry has produced incredible results in the use of e-business systems in a very short period. Supply chain, procurement, customer management systems, knowledge management, and direct sales are but a few of the programs that are in operation. Many firms are using the Internet as a vehicle to broaden their distribution and supply chains, and reach a global marketplace.

Pharmaceutical and biotech

Development and manufacturing of drugs is an expensive business. As most companies have only a set number of years where they hold exclusive manufacturing rights, they want to get to market quickly. For many years these firms have understood the value of leveraging knowledge and using electronic workgroup technology to speed the research, discovery, development and approval cycles for their operations. E-business technologies can further improve manufacturing processes, along with development of sophisticated distribution programs right to the pharmacy.

Software

This industry is a natural for e-business. Using knowledge bases to communicate with their business partners, software downloads and fixes delivered electronically, are superb tools to leverage their distribution channel; software firms have embraced e-business in a huge way.

Healthcare

Healthcare is using the Internet in some very interesting ways. At the physician level, videoconferencing, data conferencing and patient records are allowing collaboration across long distances. On-line pharmacies are opening on a regular basis and content-rich sites are building new networks in this market.

Retail

The retail market is growing, and the cost of entry is now so low that the smallest business can afford to get into the game. On-line shopping, complete with taxation and shipping software make it simple to get started. With many more shoppers on-line, the growth is sure to continue.

Telecommunications

Most of the telecommunications applications to date are in the knowledge-management and information-transfer category. Companies that are global in this space need to transfer information and software, and manage large projects across wide area networks. They are also using data marts and Internet technology to get closer to the consumer and market their services in an aggressive marketplace.

Utilities

Utility firms around the globe are facing change. Many countries are starting a program of deregulation. This means that utilities will be faced with competition in different sectors of their business operation. They will also have to undergo significant change as they move to a competitive commercial environment. E-business technology can help everywhere in the areas of maintenance, safety, sales, marketing and support of their systems.

Architecture, engineering and construction

Project management, collaboration and integration of services would all benefit from the use of e-business in an industry that continues to expand with the global economy. E-business will add a very significant collaboration tool to an industry that already uses technology for the design and support of its products and services.

Legal

The legal industry has been an electronic consumer for some time, primarily in the research zone. The Internet gives attorneys the ability to market themselves worldwide, and expand their presence and co-operation significantly. Case management across the Internet will allow firms to collaborate more effectively.

Government

Governments are committing to the Internet in a big way. Governments publish massive amounts of information and the savings in just distributing information are enormous. Many governments are also trying to improve their internal efficiency and operation. E-business is helping with this change.

Entertainment

Video, film, music and multimedia are now a major part of the Internet. As the quality of service (QoS) increase and prices for high-speed connections drop, there will be tremendous opportunities for expansion in this sector of the market.

Finance, banking and insurance

Despite a slow start, on-line banking, insurance and financial services are here to stay. In some cases, they are forcing others to change the way they operate. (Several firms have now decided to offer out-of-hours trading on the New York Stock Exchange, as some leading firms have already blazed a trail.) Many firms now want to offer a wide range of services to secure the attention of the consumers' finances, not just for banking, but also insurance, savings, retirement and estate planning.

Integrating the elements of change

With so many different angles to the issue of change, even the smartest of you may be wondering where to start. Being ready for change and understanding why it is going to happen to your industry is really the most important element.

When thinking about e-business and change, consider the following:

- technology factors;
- industry issues;
- internal culture;
- marketing strategy; and
- competition.

Despite the complex nature of these issues, you probably have a good handle on many of these already. Integrating the other factors in the development of your strategy will help you reduce risk and start to embrace change as a friend and not a foe.

There is no shortage of opportunities out there for us to pursue. We just have to think e-business, think *change*!

3

E-Business Technologies that Matter

OK, so you thought that you got away with the technology part. Sorry. This is the technology chapter. Reading this section will not make you an expert in e-business technology, but it will stop others fooling you with gobbledygook. Although the technology components are broad, the function they perform individually is not that tough to understand. This chapter will help you understand which pieces do what, and how best to apply them in your organization.

The first thing to appreciate is that no vendor has it all. Maybe IBM could provide you with more than most, but in the main, you will be dealing with different products from different vendors and suppliers. The number of relationships involved and how to manage them effectively is increasingly affecting how we think about e-business technologies.

Some basic questions can help you lay some of the technology foundations for the system. These questions will start to provide the answers to the more complex issues of information delivery, security and intranets and extranet systems.

KILLER
QUESTIONS

- What are you going to sell?
- How are you going to sell it?
- How will it be delivered?
- Are you going to sell through partners?

If you answer some of these questions, the technology components and subsequent direction will become more obvious.

Security

While security is a broad-based subject, it can be broken down into different functions based on the way that you plan to manage your business partners and customers. Although some of these systems are very complex to understand and implement, there are now many pre-packaged solutions currently available in the market, and the number of such solutions continues to expand. We can start reviewing security with one of the great strengths of the Internet, the fact that most communication is based on open standards. When it comes to security, this is its greatest flaw.

Security has several different aspects to it. Access, data, protocols, information and transactions. Most types of security systems can be broken into these various forms. Each security system involves some method of keeping the contents and information hidden from third parties who should not access these systems.

Web Hosting

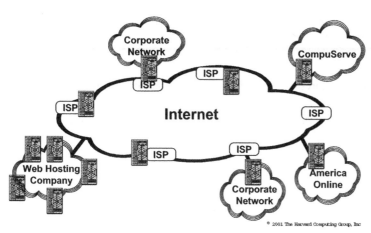

© 2001 The Harvard Computing Group, Inc

Fig. 3.1 Web-hosting security systems invariably involve firewalls.

Figure 3.1 illustrates that each of these points on the network need to be visible only to those that need to see the data, or process the transaction. Today we take much security for granted, credit card transactions in the store, at the gas station, electronic banking at the ATM, direct debits and deposits at our banks. Yet, many individuals remain concerned about security breaches and scams on, or via, the Internet. Internet security is not foolproof, but the simple act of a clerk holding my credit card while I pumped gasoline into my car recently, caused significant fraud to occur within 24 hours.

Encryption and authentication explained

Two fundamental aspects of security systems you need to understand are *encryption* and *authentication*. Each of these serves an important process in the development of secure systems.

Smart
answers to
tough
questions

Q: What is encryption?

A: Encryption is a security method to protect data from tampering by unauthorized users.

Encryption ensures that unauthorized users cannot read your data or information. The encryption process encodes the data in a way that only the
sender and the target recipient can understand. Most encryption schemes
use two components, an algorithm and a key. The algorithm is a mathemati-
cal process to "mess up" the data that needs to be protected while it is
being transferred to the target recipient. A key is then used to decode the
algorithm. The keys to "unlock" the data are made available to a different
group according to the specific application needs.

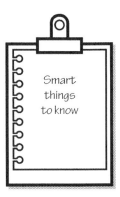

Smart
things
to know

SPOOFING

Slang for someone impersonating another on the Internet. Typically used in
electronic mail applications.

Most security systems use a combination of public and private keys to provide access to those that need to see or process the information that has
been encrypted. The public key is distributed to those individuals that you
want to send the "secure data" to, and the private key is held for you to
encrypt the message. The public key/private key scenario also has the benefit of validating that you are the person originating the transaction or the
message. (It is very easy for a hacker to "fake" your email header, thereby
creating the illusion that email was sent by someone who in fact did not
send it at all.)

They are usually stored publicly when there is a way to ensure that this level of security can be applied to multiple transaction situations.

Authentication is a method to identify that the sender and receiver of a transaction on the Internet are authorized to do so.

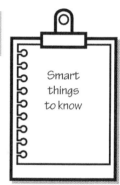

Authentication is a method to identify that the sender and receiver of a transaction on the Internet are authorized to do so. By verifying the authentic nature of the participants, a transfer or transaction may take place.

Encryption

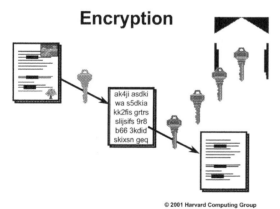

© 2001 Harvard Computing Group

Fig. 3.2 Encryption and keys at work.

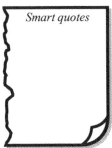
Smart quotes

"You can go and find a mailbox right now, open the door to a tin box, tin door, no lock, with unencrypted information in English, sealed in a paper-thin envelope with spit, yet people are worried about online privacy."

Scott McNealy, chairman Sun Microsystems

These basic principles provide the foundation of most Internet security systems, although they are available in a variety of forms according to the complexity and transaction needs of the e-business systems. Different types of security systems involved are listed in the table. Most systems are using these standards in one way or another (Table 3.1).

Table 3.1 Some important Internet security standards for e-business.

Standard	Function	E-business use
SSL (Secure Sockets Layer)	Provides security for the data packets at the network layer	Applications using browsers, Web servers and Internet systems
S-HTTP (Secure HTTP)	Security at the Web transaction level	Applications using browsers, Web servers and Internet systems
PGP	Provides encryption for e-mail while being transmitted across the Internet	Secure email transmission for important information
Secure MIME (S/MIME)	Security for e-mail attachments across various platforms	Secure email applications with encryption and digital signature
Secure Electronic Transaction (SET)	Security for credit card transactions	e-business payments and debits

These fundamental protocols provide the foundation for each of the systems out there in the marketplace.

A good way to picture e-business security is to view the network of computers and customers that you want to communicate with as the first stage, and then layer the business functions that are needed to make the system operational. This may not make you a security expert, but you'll be smart enough to develop a security strategy based on the way that you want your business to operate.

Many organizations are unwilling to implement secure electronic mail systems as it makes life more difficult, despite the fact that much of the content is confidential in nature. One single mistake in the email system could (probably will) send the data to the wrong individual. Many lawsuits and other problems have resulted from these simple security mishaps.

A firewall is used as a way of controlling unwanted users getting into the corporate network or intranet (Fig. 3.3). A firewall implements access con-

Firewall

A firewall is not a single entity

Usually consists of multiple software products, often running on several pieces of hardware, that provide a barrier to/from the outside world

Fig. 3.3 The firewall.

trols based on the contents of the packets of data that are transmitted between the parties and devices on the network. Valid participants are allowed in, and the firewall will provide protection against unauthorized outsiders.

Smart answers to tough questions

Q: Will a firewall protect me from virus attacks?

A: No, firewalls are designed to keep out unauthorized visitors to your systems. They do not protect against viruses. Separate software systems are needed to scan for viruses before information is transferred inside the firewall.

The word "firewall" is now often used to cover a variety of security issues, but strictly speaking, it only performs part of these functions. Use it in conjunction with other security measures such as authentication and digital signatures and you'll have a comprehensive range of access control and security systems.

By combining these elements and a secure networking protocol, companies and their partners can create Virtual Private Networks. These networks can be used as if there were physical networks, but the interconnectivity is leased from other suppliers. Another important area for Internet security is the transaction. Most of the transaction systems on the marketplace are based on technology known as Electronic Data Interchange.

Smart things to know

EDI

Electronic Data Interchange. The controlled transfer of data between businesses and organizations via established security standards.

Transactions

EDI systems provide the vehicle for input, authentication, validation, agreement and electronic payments, all to occur in seconds over the Internet. In the past it has been very expensive to implement custom EDI systems over the Internet, and therefore was limited to the larger companies who could justify the significant cost associated with the development of the system. As with many things, the Internet has made this technology accessible and affordable to everyone, including the smallest business operating from home.

SET

Secure Electronic Transmission

Smart things to know

Most financial transactions today are implemented using the SET standard. This standard is designed to allow merchant transactions to occur across the Internet. As with a traditional transaction the customer needs to have a valid account set up, then they receive a valid certificate with a public key to authenticate the transaction. Before merchants can process a transaction, they need to have certificates that contain both the bank's and their own public keys. Now we are ready to start the transaction process.

Now the cardholder starts the transaction within the store on the Internet, and the Browser authenticates the merchant from its public key. Then the customer is ready to place the order and the order is encrypted. Payment information is also encrypted, but with the bank's public key both sessions are bound together in the transaction.

Once the price and the product information are in process, the merchant verifies the customer's digital signature and then sends the order to the bank with their own certificate and payment information. At the end of the process the bank verifies the merchant's signature and payment component of the message and then authorizes payment so the merchant can fill the order.

If this seems familiar to many other "store" transactions then this should not be a surprise. It is designed to be very similar to normal "store" transactions.

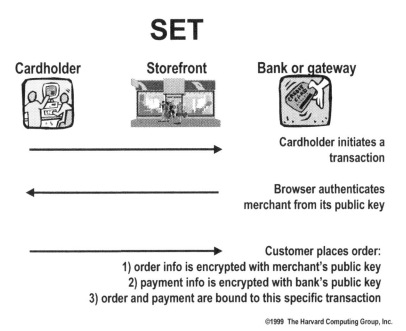

©1999 The Harvard Computing Group, Inc.

Fig. 3.4 Selected stages in a SET transaction.

Other technology groups

Most of the technology needed to develop e-business can be grouped into four categories. Application development tools are the foundation of any Web-based system. Most systems provide the technical platforms for system development and deployment. However, specialized systems have emerged into the marketplace over the last two years, dramatically reducing the time and effort needed to develop sophisticated e-business systems.

Table 3.2 Examples of technology components for e-business system selection.

Application development	Content Management	Security and transactions	Hosting and server management
Authoring tools	Managing and updating of information	Digital signatures	Bandwidth
Web servers	Version/revision control	SET	Security
Web development platforms	Personalization	Email	24 x 7
Browser	Self service applications	Inventory linking (ERP systems)	Internal/external
Network tools	International language support	Firewalls	Administration and optimization tools
Databases	Corporate Portal systems	Remote access	Remote administration
Integration tools	Information feeds and services	EDI	Monitoring and performance tools

Source: Harvard Computing Group

E-business development tools are affecting the speed at which very large-scale applications are developed. Many tools now integrate inventory management, transaction security, marketing and catalog systems. Likewise, content management systems are providing organizations with the ability to deal quickly with customization, changes and the controlled updating of sites without the need for Web authoring tools. This is particularly important for international applications that often need different language as well as content presentation to be effective.

The types of applications that are being developed include catalogs and product information sites, B2B applications, self-service and customer service applications. These applications usually require careful control and presentation of information providing the most value to the target consumer. At the same time, they also require close control of the update, release, and approval processes for the information on the site.

Authoring tools and content management

Today there are a number of tools to choose from – authoring tools ranging from the very popular visual products from Microsoft and other leading firms, right through to database-driven systems.

Most e-business systems today need to customize data and the interaction with the system. The components you must have are:

- a Web server;

- application development tools;

- a database to drive the system; and

- authoring and maintenance tools.

As the Web server is the publishing center of any e-business system, it becomes the final delivery vehicle for information input to the system. An effective way of dealing with these large volumes of data is to store the information in databases that can be accessed through the Web browser.

In many cases companies need a good way of being able to deal easily with the management, updating and modification of content inside these databases. Because of this demand Content Management Systems have emerged on the market. These systems allow for the easy modification, updating and distribution of information and tasks between different components of the e-business solution.

Content Management System purchases are driven by the need for Electronic Business or e-business. The types of applications being developed include catalogs and product information sites, business-to-business applications, self-service and customer service applications. These usually require careful control and presentation of information to provide the most value to the target consumer. At the same time they also require close control of the update, release, and approval processes for the information on the site. These systems provide information flow through the e-business solution.

Customers using Content Management Systems need control and speed. They also want quality and customization of both content and appearance. Fortunately, with the modular nature of many Content Management Systems, it is possible to have it all.

Content Management Systems provide the business controls to:

- manage the data presentation;

- enable distributed updating;

- make posting new changes fast yet customized.

How to use them

Content Management Systems provide a framework to control information. They link the authoring, approval, editing and the release (Web publishing) processes. Typically, the sorts of problems that are solved by Content Management Systems include:

- control of updates (in the hands of the content approver, not just the Webmaster);

- interactive content which keeps the Web site fresh and relevant; and

- support of the business needs of the operation by providing *control* over the customization of content for many applications and users.

Options

One decision that many firms are faced with today is whether to go with a document, publishing or business-oriented system. While for some applications the choice may not make a difference, others will clearly benefit from a particular selection. Table 3.3 illustrates some examples to help you decide.

Table 3.3 Examples of content management alternatives and where to use them.

Source: Harvard Computing Group

Customer application	Application characteristics	Best suited system
Technical publishing, database publishing, knowledge management applications	High volume electronic document applications. Built in sophisticated information retrieval and PDF generation	Document oriented Content Management
Catalogs, business-to-business applications, supply chain and distribution applications	Customization of content and presentation can be controlled interactively. Business rules can be developed and modified easily. High level of personalization.	Business oriented Content Management
Commercial publishing, electronic magazines and personalized content.	Customized content can be presented in many different forms and formats.	Publishing oriented Content Management

Knowledge management

Ask your colleagues what "e-business" means and you will get many answers. Knowledge management is the same. One way of looking at e-business systems is that they are computers that make or save money. By this definition, knowledge management systems become the food that supplies these systems.

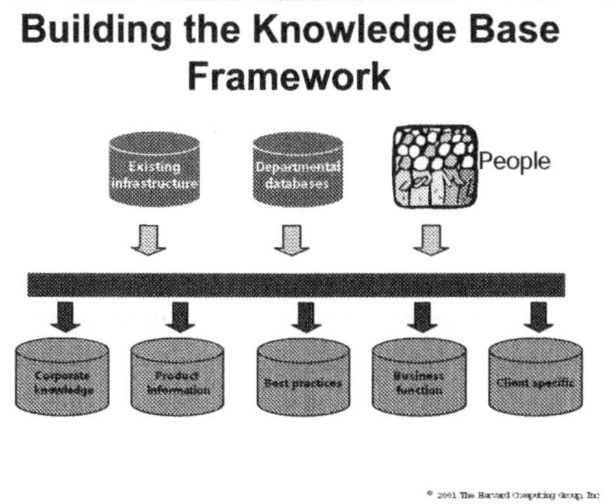

Building the Knowledge Base Framework

Fig. 3.5 Knowledge management components that can feed the e-business system.

Knowledge management systems and tools are used to capture, re-use and re-purpose the relevant information to the person that needs it, preferably at the time they need it. They can be as simple as an FAQ application, providing the right information to a client in need of on-line customer support. It could also be as complex as linking into a knowledge management repository of relevant information for a service engineer on the line. Many help-desk systems and support costs associated with them would be impossible to implement without this technology. Many KM systems are also based on groupware applications to share information between departments and individuals in the enterprise. These are usually easily integrated into e-business strategies and systems.

TOM KOULOPOULOS (AUTHOR OF *THE X-ECONOMY*)

"There is no point in responding quickly, though, if it's too late. Like a numbed hand on a hot stove, some companies may only become aware of the extent of their lack of awareness after they smell their own burning flesh."

On responding with the right information, from *The X-Economy*, Texere 2001.

Taxation

E-business systems will often use specialist software designed to calculate and segment the taxable elements of the transaction. Many vendors of e-business systems have their own taxation package, or they relicense and integrate software from vendors who specialize in this subject. Today, it is relatively easy to acquire and integrate taxation software. But take care if you are in the international marketplace that the systems chosen meet all of the collection rules and options that are permissible and required.

XML (eXtensible Markup Language)

XML is such an important standard in the development of e-business systems smart people need to know about it. XML was officially born in December 1997. The result of a working group funded by the World Wide Web consortium (W3C) and various vendors. In some ways, XML was born out of frustration, with developers and users of complex Web applications stymied by the limits of HTML. XML is now a standard that addresses many concerns. It may become the standard that finally links Web and database publishing activities in a common framework. XML has all the benefits of HTML and more. Table 3.4 illustrates the power that XML brings and if there are features that you would like to add, it's as simple as extending the language.

Table 3.4 The power and features of XML.

HTML	XML
❑ HTML describes the content of the document and no application control over presentation ❑ Usually only easily readable with a browser ❑ Non-extensible mark up ❑ No context or access control	❑ XML describes the format, presentation and provides application control over the content of the document ❑ Documents can be read, exchanged and manipulated with many applications ❑ Extensible markup language to create industry and client specific applications ❑ Context and access control

Source: ©2001 Harvard Computing Group

Database, publishing and presentation

These three primary elements influence almost all Web-based applications today. Many organizations are wrestling with the major issue of formulating a cohesive strategy for information maintenance and publishing. Those organizations on the cutting edge are having the greatest problems.

Many of the current systems developed to date, have used ODBC custom programming to produce sophisticated solutions. However, it is not a pretty sight under the covers. Most systems are hard wired to these databases, and the much-desired flexibility of platform independence is absent. XML and the associated XSL (stylesheets) could change it all.

XML provides a bridge between the publishing, database and Web presentation world in a way that has not occurred before (Table 3.5). Bridge technologies take off when market conditions demand, often as a *de facto* standard.

XML allows new things to develop that were just not previously feasible. Despite the fact that SGML defined a separate style and content model, individual controls over elements were not available to most databases to filter, manipulate or combine them. XML will make this accessible to many systems, providing parametric-based searching and reordering in the pre-

Table 3.5 Some advantages of XML.

XML	Existing industry standards
❏ Permits export of information to hard copy printable media	❏ Portable Document Format (PDF)
❏ Allows control of content based on application needs	❏ None
❏ Allows text search to be based on the context of information sought	❏ None
❏ Data oriented style and content independence	❏ SGML
❏ Centralized link management for URL updates	❏ None

Source: ©2001 Harvard Computing Group

sentation of results. The precision of the major search applications will be dramatically improved compared to today's implementations.

XML is significant because of the technical barriers it overcomes and powerful business requirements it supports. The comments below illustrate some of the adoption benefits that you can expect to happen because of the XML development currently occurring in the industry.

Smart things to say about XML

These are the business reasons for considering XML-based technology:

- we can re-use and re-purpose information quickly and efficiently;
- we can reduce the maintenance costs associated with our e-business solution;
- we can design flexibility into the system, making it easier when we want to make changes as our business requirements dictate; and
- we will be able to share information easily inside our organization and with our business partners.

Since this book was first published, XML has become the standard for business information exchange between Internet-based applications. This is so particularly for B2B applications, where specific protocols and business rules are constantly being defined and changed between different organizations.

Now that we have dealt with the major issues of where data is and how it is managed, there are a few other areas that you may want to consider to make your e-business system really fly.

Pulling technology components together

Bringing your technology components together in a common framework is not as difficult as you may think. The challenge is to ensure that you have an up to date view of the market. Each niche in the marketplace has software and hardware companies creating packaged solutions to get you to market faster. Unfortunately, there is no better way of staying current than continual monitoring of the marketplace. If you don't, you may spend more than you need on a particular solution or, even worse, be less competitive because of maintenance overheads that have been cut by innovative new technologies.

OK, you have had your fill of technology for now; let's start exploring how we can apply what we are learning. Our starting place will be one class of customers, the electronic consumer.

4

Electronic Consumers –
Attracting, Predicting
and Engaging Them

Much of the initial euphoria of the Web focused on the electronic consumer. The electronic consumer is a special type of customer for Web-based marketing. To begin with, some fundamentals of Web-based marketing will help you position your activities to best meet their needs. As the demographics of the Web have broadened, different classes of consumer have operated in various parts of it. In the early days many started out as consumers of information, which is one reason why the search sites became the primary watering hole for many of them.

During the Web's early years, from 1995 to 1998, users started at a search Web site to identify interesting places to go, specifically to find relevant information. (This continues to be a problem.) A cadre of Web sites including Yahoo!, Lycos, Excite, HotBot, AltaVista, and OpenText were the main draws at that time.

Although these sites continue to grow in popularity in terms of volume, the top ten sites drawing almost 80% of the traffic two years ago, today they are responsible for barely 50% of total Web traffic: an important change illustrating a more sophisticated use of the Web.

Who are the consumers, and where are they?

It is important to understand the demographics of the Web, particularly when you build strategies that will attract consumers. Firstly we must look at how current consumers are operating, but we must also see where the trends are leading us.

As a caveat to demographics, different sources and statistics in this book there is a wide discrepancy in numbers and estimates from the various research and consulting sources. Interestingly enough, most of the very large numbers that were predicted by researchers a couple of years ago have turned out to be relatively conservative in terms of market growth. (Something that does not normally happen with market estimates.) This just goes to show how quickly things change in this market. New products and the way that they are delivered can – and have – made new markets.

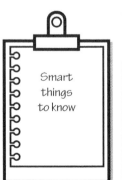

Smart things to know

In 2001, US e-commerce revenue is expected to reach $38.7 billion. Just 36% of dotcoms are pure-plays, while 63% are multi-channel businesses. Overall IT spend among dotcoms is expected to equal $15.3 billion in 2001. By 2006, when there will be an estimated 4000 dotcom companies in the United States, IT spend will decrease to $9.2 billion.

Source: Datamonitor

With a vast international community of users and potential consumers, the Internet offers an opportunity that merchants and suppliers of information and services have never seen before. Today, most users are still located in North America and Europe. However, new markets are also coming on strong as the impact of the Internet continues to grow. The numbers of users continues to expand across the globe (Table 4.1).

Table 4.1 Consumers on the Internet.

Country	Looking to purchase	Purchasing on the Internet
Australia	24%	10%
Austria	25%	12%
Belgium/Luxembourg	12%	5%
Denmark	39%	16%
Finland	28%	11%
France	12%	6%
Germany	22%	11%
Hong Kong	13%	4%
Ireland	17%	8%
Italy	10%	3%
Netherlands	28%	11%
New Zealand	29%	12%
Norway	24%	14%
Singapore	19%	7%
South Korea	18%	11%
Spain	8%	3%
Sweden	46%	26%
Switzerland	32%	17%
Taiwan	13%	4%
UK	19%	11%
United States	74%	30%

For the development of the marketplace, obviously the growth and sophistication of patterns of users will determine how quickly expansion and adoption will happen. This snapshot, taken as a Nielsen survey in June 2001, illustrates the high percentage of populations now gaining on-line access and increasing the buying activities. This will ultimately provide the foundation for the growth of the industry.

The most popular activities of users continue to be email, finding information about a hobby, and general news. These continue to outrank on-line shopping as an activity. However, on-line shopping is growing in popularity. As it becomes easier to facilitate the delivery of goods and services using the Internet and associated overnight shipment services, the convenience of shopping on the Internet is catching on fast.

Services that would not have been considered reasonable to purchase a few years ago are becoming popular. However most of the sales to date are in books, CDs, software, high tech and other items that are easy to shop for and deliver to the consumer. The range of offerings is likely to expand dramatically as groceries, financial services and even on-line house hunting expand their current small penetration of the marketplace.

Table 4.1 shows for the first time some softening in the retail marketplace on the Web, particularly in the greater penetration that has occurred in the North American marketplace. However the outlook for e-commerce still looks rosy over the long term.

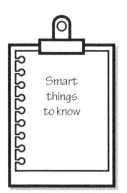

Smart
things
to know

EARLY ADOPTERS

Group of consumers that start using technology and systems early in their introduction to the marketplace.

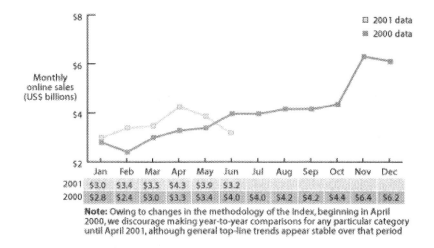

	Jan	Feb	Mar	Apr	May	Jun	Jul	Aug	Sep	Oct	Nov	Dec
2001	$3.0	$3.4	$3.5	$4.3	$3.9	$3.2						
2000	$2.8	$2.4	$3.0	$3.3	$3.4	$4.0	$4.0	$4.2	$4.2	$4.4	$6.4	$6.2

Note: Owing to changes in the methodology of the Index, beginning in April 2000, we discourage making year-to-year comparisons for any particular category until April 2001, although general top-line trends appear stable over that period

Fig. 4.1 Sample demographics of the Internet and e-business in North America. Courtesy of Forrester Research.

With more than 170 million Internet users in the US alone, and an estimated 471 million worldwide, the marketplace has exploded to provide a very high level of actual and potential business for merchants. At the same time, the expansion in offerings of different types of products and services has made it very attractive for many consumers to become enamored with the opportunity and convenience of shopping on-line.

Smart things to say

With a market of approaching 500 million worldwide, as Internet users turn to Internet shoppers and consumers, huge changes in purchasing patterns will occur.

Users are becoming more sophisticated and are moving on from the first typical applications that attracted them to the Internet, typically email and Web browsing for research.

Table 4.2 Combined home and work access of the Internet

Average Internet Use in June 2001 Combined home and work access			
	June	May	% Change
Number of sessions per month	32	31	0%
Number of unique sites visited	21	21	0%
Page views per month	1,114	1,109	0.5%
Page views per surfing session	35	35	0%
Time spent per month	16:29:14	16:31:02	-0.2%
Time spent during surfing session	0:31:02	0:30:27	1.9%
Duration of page view	0:00:53	0:00:53	-0.8%
Active Internet universe (actually surfed)	112.9 million	113.7 million	-0.8%
Current Internet universe	173.6 million	173.6 million	-0.0%
Source: Nielsen//NetRatings			

The trends shown above also indicate that more and more users are not just browsing or using email, but are in fact shopping on the Internet. Of those 55 million that are shopping, more than half (28 million) are buying as well.

Recent polls taken show the typical applications and activities of digital consumers, and have shown the following buying patterns.

Buying habits of 2400 "digital consumers" over recent 90-day period:

- 41% participated in an on-line auction;
- 26% bought computer software;
- 25% banked on-line;
- 25% bought books;
- 23% bought airline tickets;
- 12% made hotel or travel arrangements; and
- 12% traded stocks, bonds or mutual funds.

Smart things to say

Many consumers continue to visit on-line stores and locations to ensure that they effectively research their purchases before they are made. As more organizations offer exacting information about products and services, the Web is becoming the location of choice to find purchase information.

CONSUMERS

While many consumers are still making their purchases in a "bricks and mortar" store, much of the research and decision-making process is being done on-line in advance of the process.

Smart things to say

Keeping an eye on consumer groups and trends

Many firms have spent a lot of money watching what has been happening in the marketplace, and are then adjusting their strategy accordingly. On the Internet, you need to be a little more aggressive and predictive. You don't want to miss out totally on a new trend or class of buyer in the marketplace.

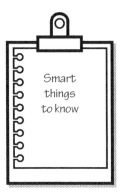

PLANNED E-COMMERCE SPENDING

Spending	
$1–50	31%
$51–100	24%
$101–200	14%
$201–500	18%
more than $500	12%
Frequency	
Once a week or more	11%
Every two or three weeks	19%
Once a month	33%
Every two months	14%
Every three months	20%
Less often	4%
Source: Yahoo!/ACNielsen	

The fact that many of the research firms have been incorrect in their assumptions about the e-business marketplace underlines the need to watch the market. Understand the demographics and buying patterns in your market and let them impact your e-strategy.

Smart
things
to know

Keeping up to speed with consumer trends

Observing industry trends on the Internet is an effective way ensuring that you do not miss out on big opportunities. As we'll see later, it's risky to do nothing but watch the market develop and then come in when some buying patterns and demand are in place.

To stay up with industry trends, try the following:

- subscribing to leading industry magazines;
- visiting the Internet research sites regularly; and
- subscribing to industry-specific newsletter and newsgroups.

SMART THINGS
TO DO

Retaining and engaging consumers

Building a client base that will meet your needs on the Web is obviously "first base" for any strategy involving digital consumers. Once you have established the prospects for your product, test the market, particularly if you plan to make this a mainstream initiative for your company.

In general, companies look at the Web in two ways. Firstly, to find a way of better dealing with their current clientele, and secondly, to expand their base significantly. When reviewing ways to achieve both goals, the tactics and techniques outlined will be useful for either case. However, the amount of energy expended, and the potential costs associated with the latter option could be very significant.

Much of what has been learned about Web customers draws on experience of traditional means of acquiring and managing relationships. It costs lots of money to gain the first customer, and once you have them and can keep them satisfied, they are likely to come back. No rocket science here. However, when you apply many of the bulk marketing techniques common to US and European marketing strategies, some bad things happen. By working the percentages, we assume that we will have results based on volume and filtering of potential prospects. Consequently, we tend to use familiar media mechanisms such as direct mail and telemarketing, targeting a group that will meet certain demographic criteria such as:

- company size;

- demographics;

- industry;

- title and decision-making profile; and

- a user of product that would make them a prospect.

Our tendency is to filter these results, based on this process, until we end up with a number of "qualified leads" to go to the next stage. These leads are often handled by internal sales teams on the telephone, and then forwarded to field account reps for appointments to be held (or they could be handled directly on the telephone, dependent on the product or service).

Consequently, we lean to this approach of targeting, contacting, filtering, distributing and then following up accordingly. If we lived in an ideal world, the following would not transpire:

- we would not send unsolicited mail that would either not reach, or would annoy the recipient;

- more of the "follow up" calls would occur at the right time in the sales cycle;

- we would not "lose leads" because we did not have the staff to follow up on them;

- field sales staff would not "cherry pick" the leads they wanted; and

- if we target the wrong user, or provide them with the inappropriate product the process fails.

Smart
things
to know

PUSH

Delivery of information to potential consumers via electronic means.

Unfortunately, we all know that this does happen and does so on a regular basis. Most of what we have described could be considered a "push" marketing effort. Although we tend to consider *push* as something that is a Web phenomenon, we have in fact been pushing the same stuff to prospects and clients alike for many years. Now we understand some of the problems with our traditional marketing approach, we can review what excites consumers on the Internet. Let's consider the alternatives for the consumer on the Internet and why the way we contact them is important:

Smart things to say

Internet consumers:

- can slam the door on you without you knowing;
- can leave the room quickly;
- can leave the room quietly;
- are likely to tell others about their experience; and
- will tell more people if the experience is negative.

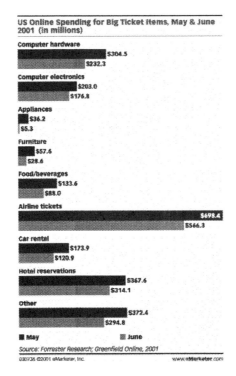

US Online Spending for Big Ticket Items, May & June 2001 (in millions)

Computer hardware: $304.5 / $232.3

Computer electronics: $203.0 / $176.8

Appliances: $36.2 / $5.3

Furniture: $57.6 / $28.6

Food/beverages: $133.6 / $88.0

Airline tickets: $698.4 / $566.3

Car rental: $173.9 / $120.9

Hotel reservations: $367.6 / $314.1

Other: $372.4 / $294.8

■ May   ▒ June

Source: Forrester Research; Greenfield Online, 2001

030736 ©2001 eMarketer, Inc.   www.eMarketer.com

Fig. 4.2 On-line spending trends, summer 2001. (Source: Forrester Research)

In Cyberspace, clients can close the door and slam the phone down very fast. Patience is not something that many consumers have on the Internet. Understanding what makes them excited and what turns them off in this very short timeframe is obviously critical to success. One thing for sure is that we know that Internet consumers love good content. If the content is good, then they are likely to stay and see more of what you have to offer. If the content is bad, unless there is some other tremendous reason to be on your site, they are likely not just to leave, but are very unlikely to return. As most companies and organizations are trying to find ways to get people to go to the site in the first place, if they "bail out" quickly once they are there, all that marketing effort has been for naught.

Content is king. Study after study continues to emphasize this as the number one factor.

CONTENT

- *Good content is the #1 reason people return to Web sites.*
- *75% of 8600 respondents cited content as the reason for return visits.*
- *Other reasons for return visits included ease of use, quick download time, and frequent updates.*

Source: Forrester Research

Smart things to say

Understanding who is visiting your site and why is vital to your strategy. There are different types of visitors – customers, prospects, partners and the press. It is important that each of these has a fulfilling experience. Determining which ones are most important and how best to make this experience have useful outcomes for your business will start you on the right road for development of your Web environment.

As I keep saying, recalling your business goals and linking them to the experience of visiting the site: this will help.

Attracting potential customers is one thing. Retaining them is another. You must encourage consumer loyalty. This is not something that can be done as a part of a simple Web marketing effort. Rather it has to be built into the fabric of sales and marketing efforts. Building this type of loyalty can be very effective for the development of a long-term effective strategy on the Web.

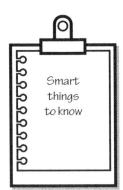

Smart things to know

GOOD CONTENT

The number one reason why people return to Web sites.

Smart quotes

"Content is what will determine long-term Internet profitability. To focus on technology without content is like building a hospital without nurses and doctors."

Ed Horowitz, who heads up Citigroup's e-Citi division

This type of program will replace the "event" marketing so common to early Web efforts. Many firms will promise a high level of traffic in a short period, but what use will this be if your consumers "bail out" after a short time on the site?

Here are some good ideas to assist with the development of loyalty from your e-business site.

- *Create value.* When someone visits your site give him or her something of value. Creating value is one of the most important aspects to create loyalty. It provides a reason for returning and can be very simple. Offer redeemable coupons or rebates to consumers, and make them available only on your Web site. Airlines have been using this to great effect in their craving to get consumers to sign up and purchase tickets on-line. Moreover, it is working. In the US there are many fares that are only available via the Web, and sometimes at a much lower cost than the traditional travel agent can offer.

- *Convenience.* Make your site easier than anywhere else. Even purchasing an automobile, can now be made easier on the Web. Information sites such as carpoint.com have almost as much (in some cases more) information about cars than you can find on the automakers' own Web sites. TicketMaster, a supplier of concert and event tickets has increased its Web presence and revenue considerably over the past year. This is most certainly due to the tremendous convenience of this service. In addition to the ease of signing up and getting information on the Web, there are usually no telephone lines or operators to wait for, all of which contribute to an experience of convenience.

- *Confidence.* Building confidence for your visitors is a good method to improve traffic and loyalty. If a brand is already established, such as the *Wall Street Journal*, there is not much work required to make that translate to the Web environment. But new brands and sites need to build the confidence of their users before they will return time and again.

- *Entertainment value.* Creating entertainment also offers a good way of bringing consumers back. Sometimes this can be as simple as a joke of the day. JellyBelly.com offers an on-line survey at its Web site that users have to come back to the site to participate in at various times of the day. As the time changes each day, consumers have to keep coming back to try to get to the survey and win the free samples.

- *Customer service.* Outstanding customer service for your consumer is one of the most important aspects of any e-business experience. Last year, our consulting firm purchased an enterprise network computer via an on-line auction, egghead.com. The server arrived within the five days advertised, but unfortunately without a critical circuit board that was part of the original order. The total order was for around $2500 but the component that was missing had a cost of around $2000. (It was a good deal!). The company also found that they were out of stock of the item. The resolution? Egghead.com told us to purchase the item directly from the manufacturer and then reimbursed us with a credit to our account. This type of service, even when you obviously lose money on this sale, creates confidence and loyalty that runs beyond any single deal.

Customer service may now become the biggest differentiation for many operations. Consumers have many ways that they can find out the "best price" for their sales, but still the creation of "great service" will create loyalty beyond just the issue of price.

Targeted marketing strategies

Development of your own targeted marketing strategy to address consumer needs is a great way to gain the results you want and avoid the problems. You can use targeted marketing strategies and techniques to make this happen.

Because the consumer base is huge on the Web, and the cost of reaching it is low, you need a targeted marketing strategy.

eMarketing Roadmap

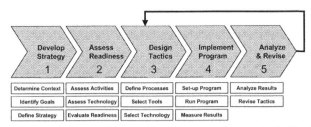

Fig. 4.3 E-marketing programs provide an excellent method of building communities of interested prospects and leads. © 2001 The Harvard Computing Group, Inc.

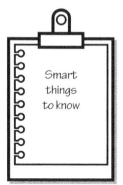

EMAIL

Electronic mail is the least expensive method of targeting information to meet a specific prospects profile.

Targeted marketing programs align the needs of specific sectors of the market with exact matches for the product or service that you plan to present. In recent years, these sorts of programs have become very popular. One of the major reasons is the lower cost of obtaining and retaining clients.

And the basic marketing costs endorse these strategies. Email remains by far the most cost-effective way of delivering a message to potential clients. A customized message can be delivered for around $0.05 per unit. Compare these costs with direct mail at somewhere between $2–5 dollars, and between $8–24 for telephone marketing.

Smart things
to say

Compare these contact costs:

- electronic mail $0.05 per unit;
- direct mail $2–5 per unit;
- telephone interview and contact $8–24; and
- face-to-face interview $40–400.

Of all of these, the face-to-face interview is the most expensive. Therefore the better the qualification earlier in the process, the better the chance we have of producing sales that are more suited to the business situation. Targeted marketing can dramatically cut the cost of sales, while at the same time reducing the time taken to complete the sale. The Internet is a very effective way of cutting prospecting.

Start a targeted marketing program by segmenting and test marketing the potential client base. This will give you information related to the target consumer and how best to reach them via various Internet and marketing programs.

Once you have selected the target base, think about the following ways to get to it.

Direct email

Direct email with a customized message is one of the most effective ways of delivering information to your potential targets. Today there are a myriad of tools and programs out there to help you with the development of your targeted program.

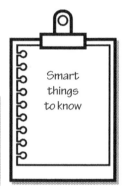

Smart things to know

> **SPAMMING**
>
> The indiscriminate sending of large amounts of junk email to a very broad audience, knowing that a large number of the consumers will not want to receive it.

It is important not to confuse targeted email and "spam." Spammers, next to confidence tricksters and pedophiles, are rated in the top categories of hated operatives on the Internet. You do not want to be a member of this group. The "junkmail" that they produce is the scourge of Internet Service Providers, hosting services and corporate MIS departments around the world. Development of email programs should always meet the privacy standards and be respectful of the organizations email policies. (Many firms have very good screening software that will stop email coming in from a particular domain name if you do not comply.)

Smart things
to say

DIRECT EMAIL PROGRAMS

- Select a list that has the target names and positions that you need.
- Develop the copy carefully.
- Allow users to "remove" themselves from any targeted email list.
- Allow other users to easily "subscribe" to lists, so that email can be forwarded to interested parties.
- If you are going to make this part of a series to a target base, try and automate the process using e-mail marketing programs and services.
- HTML mail systems can help include graphics and a more personalized version of the materials.
- Never use "spam" methods.

Building your own email list, and using an email mail list server can be a great way of ensuring that consumers proactively subscribe to offers and information about your products without a lot of sales effort. A significant community of interested parties can be built in a relatively short period, and users can add or remove themselves without the need for much maintenance in the process. This self-policing method is non-intrusive and avoids putting people off before you start any form of business relationship with them.

Bulletin boards, newsgroups and threaded discussion groups

Another effective method of creating sales and general interest in a product or service is the bulletin board or threaded discussion group. Users can proactively sign up for more information or a specific service.

In today's climate it is reasonable to allow visitors to a site to decide if they want to be added to another list as a result of participating in a discussion group. Naturally you need to maintain the privacy of each member of these groups. Most professional or hobby bulletin boards and related Newsgroups specifically request that members do no soliciting. However, less scrupulous companies and individuals often ignore these requests. A good rule of thumb is to treat each one of these areas just as you would want to be treated yourself.

Smart things to know

ROBOTING

Capturing Internet demographic information about visitors to sites, which are equipped with technology to acquire data on the visitor.

Roboting and gathering intelligence on Web visitors

Robots are yet another way to gain information on consumers. When a visitor to a site clicks on a certain section, system monitoring software will capture the location of where the visitor has come from. In many cases much more information than this can be collected, including email addresses.

Most organizations now use technology that will help understand how many visitors they have, where they have come from, how long they stayed and which path they took through the site. Web information systems and tools provide this for most sites on the marketplace. However, when a visitor is roboted, then information including their email address can then be used to create automated email to provide automated "follow up" to the visit. This can be a very powerful tool if used appropriately. I recommend that you make it clear the privacy standards that your site and organization uses. You may want to consider an "opt-in" policy for mailing lists and other information.

Other traffic-building techniques

Increasing Web traffic always remains one of the top items to consider for the success of an e-business site. After all, we know that creating Web traffic is not purely a "build it and they will come" slam dunk.

Build Web traffic through:

- appropriate registration at the search engines;
- content partnerships;
- banner advertising;
- press relations; and
- Web-based events.

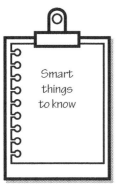

SPIDER

A tool to automate the registration of your site with popular search engines to ensure that your content is indexed by them on their next visit.

A combination of these programs will build the traffic on your site. The simplest of all is to register with search engines. There is no question that many Internet consumers still rely on a major search engine or portal to help them find the things they are looking for. We have all been spammed to death by companies and services offering to make us number one on the results list for fees ranging from $50 on up. Marketing companies offer these services on a continuous basis. Acquiring a spider to assist with the placement and registration of your site to the larger search engines is also a worthwhile expense. Many of the software products that the professionals use at Internet Service Providers and marketing firms are available to the public for a very modest fee.

Another method is RealNames.™ You can purchase these keywords on the Web via the realnames.com Web site. They avoid the need for www prefixes on Web sites, and allow users that have their browser plug in to go directly to their target site. In the long term, this could become a very popular method of navigating, and attracting consumers to your site. If you purchase the right to a "RealName" you can link it directly to the appropriate part of your Web site. For example if you were working for Ford Motors, you could acquire Ford Explorer as a RealName, and then type the key words "Ford Explorer" on your browser. You would then be directed specifically to that Web page, with no HTML address needed.

Smart things to know

IMPRESSION

A single view of an element of a Web page. Often referred to for advertising measurements on the Web when each impression represents the presentation and viewing of an on-line advertisement.

Content Partnerships

Banner Advertising

Search Engines

Email Advertising

Press Relations

Web-based Events

© 2001 The Burned Computing Group, Inc

Fig 4.4 Example of traffic-building techniques.

A content partnership is another great way to improve the quality of the consumer experience on your site, as good content can keep them coming back. Combine this with a community strategy to create real interest in your site.

Smart things to know

Advertising is one more way of driving traffic to your site if you know where your prospects are going. Today most advertising is still operating on a CPM basis. Dependent on the site, it could cost you anywhere from $25–75 per thousand impressions. Unfortunately, this does not guarantee that others will actually click on this advertisement and thereby come to your site, it just means they will see the ad. Due to a relatively low click-thru rate, it is likely that more and more advertisers will be more discerning and move to either more specialized sites where higher click-thrus are likely, or start paying for advertising on a different basis.

Some advertising firms are now starting to offer advertising based on the number of click-thrus to the advertiser site. Although the price will be considerably higher for this option, it is likely that more advertisers will start to move in this direction. Web-based events also keep users coming back for more at your site. Try competitions, delivery of reports, seminars and other useful programs that will help make the visit worthwhile.

Press relations are another way of making the site an interesting place to go. Investors, analysts, consultants and clients are often curious to know how things are going. Press releases can also be an unobtrusive way of delivering news without being too obvious.

Relationship marketing

With target marketing and the technology available in the marketplace, you are now ready to start relationship marketing.

RELATIONSHIP MARKETING

Relationship marketing can create a community of interested parties in your product or service.

Smart things to say

Relationship marketing comprises many components including, one-to-one marketing, personalization, communities, customization and customer relationship management (CRM). (As an all-embracing term, CRM probably describes the entire process most completely; here we are dealing only with marketing aspects of this process, and not the total customer management experience.)

Relationship marketing will allow you to do incredible feats on the Internet. Never before have we had the opportunity to make up totally new ways of accessing consumers and prospects, while at the same time fine-tuning the message and product according to their needs.

RELATIONSHIP MARKETING AND E-BUSINESS

Relationship marketing on the Internet allows to you present your offerings in a very personalized way, impossible with traditional means, or traditional costs.

Smart things to say

Customization

Customizing content is one very effective way of ensuring that the right information can be presented to the right group at the right time. With earlier versions of software and systems on the market, this was a very difficult process. As all of the systems that provide customized content capabilities are database-driven, providing many different versions of the same materials and still maintaining performance that met the user needs was very difficult. Today, however, there are many systems that allow this to occur quickly and easily. For applications where the same data is being presented to different audiences (such as information feeds, catalogs and knowledge-management applications), customization becomes a way of life.

Smart things to say

RELATIONSHIP MARKETING

Relationship marketing offers a unique method of customizing product offering around a particular consumer's needs.

It can also be very useful dealing with the different locations of consumers, who may be in different geographic locations or even speaking different languages. Many companies operating in different locations offer customization options as consumers enter their site. The experience in the site is then customized to their language, product, pricing and support needs in this target marketplace.

Personalization

Personalization takes customization to the next stage. It builds marketing messaging and Web pages based on individuals' specific personal needs.

Software to offer this capability has reached new heights in terms of personalization. This can include development of Web pages that contain the specific product information based on your buying patterns, previous visits through the site and how long you stayed in a particular area.

RELATIONSHIP MARKETING

Relationship marketing offers a great way to personalize the shopping and buying experience.

Smart things to say

Many individuals perceive that they are being watched while they are out there on the Web. They are right, and companies are paying more and more attention to consumer patterns. While this smacks to some of Big Brother, you could argue that you would not let someone else come into your house without watching them as they pass through.

Personalization tools allow Web merchants and content providers to deliver, for example, individual versions of *PC Week* to your desktop, as well as customized auction items and complete sets of products that are specifically focused on your needs.

Community building

Creating communities on the Web has become a popular pastime recently. For a good reason. This is a great way of providing interesting content, relevant to your potential client base, and then offering your products as part of the experience.

Q: Why will a community help my Web strategy?

A: Communities are a great way of providing the interesting and useful content to my potential buyers, partners and influencers in our sales strategy.

Earlier in this chapter we reviewed that *content* was king. Many organizations have recognized the value of a community for their clients and prospects, and are making money as a result.

Smart things
to say

Include the following in your community-building program:

- email newsletters;
- reports relevant to the industry;
- community calendars;
- public bookmark files;
- chat events;
- promotions and contests;
- community forums and bulletin board; and
- community knowledge bases.

A good community site will allow customers to feel unthreatened and to visit repeatedly to receive useful information relevant to their task and focus. These can be hobby sites, professional or focused around other vertical applications or areas of interest.

Developing an effective community site can reduce your customer acquisition costs over the long haul. However, the cost of developing the community site can be considerable in the initial stages, particularly as you will

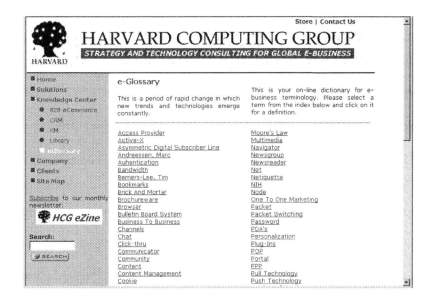

Fig. 4.5 An example of a community-focused site. Courtesy Harvard Computing Group, Inc.

likely have to purchase some content outside the company to keep it interesting. In addition to the benefit of lower customer acquisition costs, your credibility will also increase. (Providing useful information to your clients will help to establish credibility.)

One-to-one marketing

Since the first edition of this book, the entire concept of one-to-one marketing has moved from leading-edge marketing to consumers, to a much more common method of doing business. You should not be surprised that the earlier elements in this chapter are used extensively in development of a one-to-one marketing strategy. One-to-one allows companies to focus their efforts to really target their client base with the products that are the best match for each consumer with an offer they should be unable to refuse. It also personifies the very best of customer retention and management over a long-cycle relationship with them, receiving input and opinions over time and re-using them to the best effect for the company.

Whichever strategies you decide to use for your client base, there is no shortage of tools, assistance and companies that can help in the process. The practices and programs outlined here should help you get pointed in the right direction.

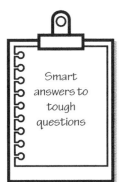

Smart answers to tough questions

Q: What is one-to-one marketing?

A: Customization and personalization of your product and prospect's requirements to meet an individual set of established needs. Once matched, a one-to-one marketing program delivers an exact marketing message, with the appropriate product to meet the prospect's needs.

Affiliate programs

Many marketing programs cannot be built without considering affinity programs. Amazon almost invented this category on the Web, with their program starting in 1996; this allowed others to place Amazon logos and products on their Web site. Their goal was to create click-thrus to their site, leading to purchases being made on their site. Their current program how has a membership of close to 250,000 members.

Affinity programs are estimated to already generate reference sales of around 13% of all e-business sales in retail today. Industry watchers, Forrester Research, expect this to reach 21% by 2003. They also rate higher in e-business effectiveness, well ahead of e-mail, PR, and other traditional media methods. A recent study by Harvard Computing Group draws comparisons between the very successful franchise models in the fast-food industry and today's electronic "franchising of the brand" through affinity programs. Time will tell if this is a reasonable comparison, but there is no question that these programs can assist a business dramatically.

Q: What is an affinity program?

A: An affinity program is a partnership between Web sites. The Web site owner that has developed the program is called the "sponsor" and the user of the program is the "host" or "target" site.

Smart answers to tough questions

Affinity programs are partnerships between Web sites. The Web site owner that has developed the program is called the "sponsor" and the user of the program is the "host" or "target" site. Examples such as Amazon make it easy to understand how effective these programs are and how well they scale. Amazon builds its affinity program, and then affinity partners sign up and receive payment in return for sales that are generated via site referrals (click thrus) or banner advertising links.

These are often compared to Web advertising models that pay host sites a fixed fee-per-view (CPM) or click-thru to the sponsor site. Some sites will use programs that are similar to paid affinity programs, for example not-for-profits, professional associations and other certification endorsements. These programs can often follow similar self-service models, similar in all but the payment element of the program.

Affinity programs continue to evolve with the marketplace. As the Web has evolved, so has the basic affinity program model. Changes include:

- *Syndicated e-commerce.* In the past, shoppers and visitors were passed through to the sponsor's site via the "click thru" model. They would then place the order once at the destination. A syndicated model allows users to remain at the visiting site, by facilitating "a store" at their site. By keeping the users at the host's site, greater "stickiness" is achieved, as the visitor has no need to leave the site to complete the transaction.

  An example of this model is Nexchange, which provides stores for their syndicated clients. By providing the shops on the hosting site, the look and feel of the member's Web site can be maintained, and their clients are automatically returned to the originating Web site once the shopping transaction is complete. This will appear seamless to the end user.

- *Corporate intranets.* B2B affiliate programs, using corporate intranets as the target, are rapidly becoming popular. This allows others to participate in revenue sharing by placing links to the company's suppliers on the corporate intranet. By offering these links, companies can give employees preferred discounts by these arrangements, and facilitate the use of products from specific companies who are known or preferred suppliers. Programs such as those from Linkshare allow these programs to be implemented, and then track activities resulting from the program.

- *International programs.* Affinity programs are growing in popularity in the international marketplace. Firms like PlugInGo.com have established a presence in Europe, and Be Free has built a relationship with the media giant Bertelsmann.

  Intermediaries and brokers who are providing the services to track the sales and pay out commissions to affiliates are further facilitating the international programs. Similar to the Web advertising world, firms wanting to sponsor these programs do not have to set up the technology to deal with the hosting and tracking of activities. Companies such as LinkShare.com and Refer-it.com can provide these facilities.

Why affinity programs make sense

Affinity programs continue to grow in popularity as both sponsor and host site benefit from the relationship. The advantages to the sponsor include:

- increased sales with relatively low acquisition cost;

- increases in the sponsor's visibility in the market;

- leveraged distribution model; and

- expansion of the business network, creating new connections via self-service means.

Firms and organizations that are using host affinity programs benefit considerably. Benefits include:

- cash compensation for traffic and leads driven from the site;

- commissions from sales derived as a result of the program;

- improved brand awareness; and

- an increase in the "stickiness" of the site.

Future trends in affinity programs

These programs continue to have explosive growth, and expansion across many markets will continue in the coming years.

The traditional development of these systems has been based on the one-to-many model. Allowing sponsors to create programs that are then delivered to large numbers of end user customers has been the model of choice. While this works well in the B2C market, it can also be used effectively in a reverse situation, particularly for applications such as e-procurement and the like.

As organizations continue to become frustrated at the ineffectiveness of Web-based advertising, affiliate programs and how they are deployed will become more creative. Because e-marketing programs such as e-mail and newsletter are outrunning print and Web-based advertising, sponsors are looking for new ways to get their message out there. New destinations will be targets, such as internal sponsorships on e-procurement and Electronic Bill and Presentation Systems (EBPS).

Electronic Bills are rapidly becoming the focus of many of these processes, including their print media brethren. Other locations and means to deliver these affiliate programs will test the creativity of marketers everywhere.

One-to-many model

In the B2B world, most goods are not sourced by surfing the Web. Most products are acquired through negotiated contracts with qualified suppliers or some spot market is identified to fulfill the need. Also, as many products purchased by businesses are components or unfinished goods, the B2C, one-to-many model does not have the same attraction as the consumer market.

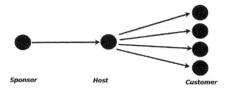

Sponsor   Host   Customer

© 2001 The Harvard Computing Group, Inc

Fig. 4.6 The one-to-many model.

As a result, most business customers are likely to do their buying at a few predefined sites. These sites are likely to offer complementary content and have the potential of a many-to-many relationship. This will, in effect, create the conditions for expansion of an organization's business network.

As merchants continue to search for ways to reach the market effectively, new programs will emerge in this market. The connection between an interested and engaged consumer and their aversion to Web advertising continues to vex Web marketers. However new affiliate marketing models, with syndicated content and product information, will likely supplant the traditional advertising programs.

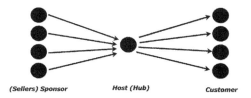

(Sellers) Sponsor   Host (Hub)   Customer

© 2001 The Harvard Computing Group, Inc

Fig. 4.7 The many-to-many model illustrating new characteristics of B2C programs.

These new e-commerce networks will combine media and seller sites with exclusive content to create differentiated and unique selling opportunities. Forrester Research has recently completed studies on this topic, often referred to as "elastic retailing." As the range of products and services on the Web continues to expand, the development of self-service applications that support these environments is sure to be rapid. This is particularly so where differentiation between many product offerings is hard to discern, a point further illuminated by shopping agents such as MySimon.

Content remains king

Understanding the value of content to Web sites has moved from desirable to mandatory. Most organizations, particularly partner-oriented firms, understand this deeply. However, creating and delivering this compelling content is key to the success of affinity programs. Keeping a site "sticky" is critical to its success, and many organizations are turning to content syndicators to acquire the content to leverage and support traffic on their sites. Others are commissioning or developing original content to attract and keep visitors coming back for more. Firms such as ScreamingMedia and iSyndicate are specializing in these areas.

So, determining how and when you are going to attract and keep electronic consumers – and make the relationship work – turns out to be more complex that just putting up the Web page and licensing the software for the store.

Some research and clear understanding of the target audience and how you are going to reach them in a consistent and profitable manner needs careful thought. The good news is that there are lots of consumers out there, and more are buying directly from the Web. As the confidence of Internet consumers increases, and broader services are offered, the opportunity is clear. There are customers out there. All you have to do is find them, interest them, convince them, sell them and then retrain them.

5

B2B – Business-to-Business E-Business (It's Not Just About Consumers)

Most e-business noise in the news is about the business-to-consumer market. As we reviewed in Chapter 2 this is small potatoes compared with what is happening in the business-to-business (B2B) e-business market. This market is a giant, and one with a very big appetite for growth.

Business-to-business (B2B)

Business-to-business is all about transactions between your operations and partners that can help your operations. Any transactions and information associated with making, delivering, selling and supporting products or services can be candidates for a B2B system. This broad definition includes many different systems that can improve the communications between companies and organizations.

BUSINESS-TO-BUSINESS (B2B)

The use of the Internet and electronic networks that effects transactions between business operations and their partners in marketing, sales, development, manufacturing and support. This is the largest segment of the Internet, and the fastest growing.

Industries have been using business-to-business strategies and processes to support the development of their products, services and partnerships. For example, the aerospace industry has been working with partners in the airframe, avionics and engine categories. Each member of these supply-chain groups co-ordinates design, development, testing, acceptance, production and maintenance schedules.

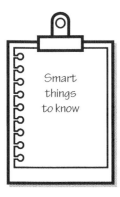

EFT

Electronic Funds Transfer. The secure transfer of funds via an agreed protocol and system.

The automotive industry has developed some major initiatives, including the joint e-business supply-chain program with Ford, GM, Chrysler and Renault. The COVISNT exchange could eventually facilitate more than $260 billion dollars in annual purchases and 120,000 suppliers in a single system.

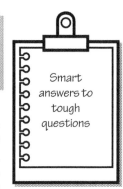

Smart answers to tough questions

The today's banking and finance operations have long been dependent on EDI and EFT to ensure that monies and securities are transferred to the company or individual that requested the action. Product manufacturers, such as engineering firms, have used business-to-business project management, manufacturing and outsourcing for the development and delivery of their products.

It is likely that you are already using some form of business-to-business system in your organization. Many systems including office suppliers, on-line travel agents and information services, are on-line businesses. Some of these have been spectacularly successful.

SMART COMPANIES: TRAVELOCITY.COM

One such company is Travelocity.com a provider and leader in the on-line travel business. Their rapidly growing business-to-business strategy has won them several awards for service and results. By developing a site that has registered more than 28.7 million users, the company created loyalty and meteoric sales growth. Their business clients have on-line access to most airlines, 50,000 hotels, and over 50 car rental firms.

Smart things to know

Supply-chain management systems make it possible for participants in the supply chain to see where the production, supply and inventory are in the process. For years, high-tech organizations have been using these business-to-business systems as a way of connecting teams spread about the globe.

This has led to the development of *electronic immigration*, with outsourced teams of professionals all using a common system. Before the Internet, making connections between these locations required private networks for the groups of collaborators in these business-to-business chains. Despite this cost, the benefits were large enough to warrant large investments in network infrastructure. Companies and organizations set up these private networks, which were developed to support these business-to-business activities.

However, without the Internet or some common communications vehicle, the cost of setting these up was high, therefore only the most critical systems were implemented.

Then came the Internet, and things started to change. Companies and organizations set up their own domain names, email servers and supporting systems. As they did so, the communication traffic and patterns between businesses began to change. Your organization is probably already seeing the benefit of using these electronic tools. They have allowed us to create documents and internal communication using email. This has now become

Timeframe to publish and update

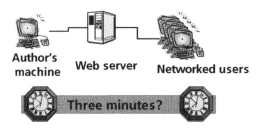

©1999 The Harvard Computing Group, Inc.

Fig. 5.1 Example of business-to-business benefits of on-line information publishing.

Smart
things
to know

a natural extension to use the same tools for email and transmission of documents between our existing and potential partners and clients.

After a while it became obvious that some of the other functions used by some of the techies in the organizations, such as FTP and chat, were extremely useful and relevant to business-to-business users. The ability to broadcast large amounts of information and changes to a large number of people improved operations considerably.

The logical step for us was to extend these systems to our business partners, and yet exclude the general public. This caused a new network to emerge. This secure business-to-business network provides the foundation of the Internet business-to-business growth.

Smart quotes

"Recognizing the need for an e-business model is the slam dunk; finding the *right* model is the challenge."

Brian Gillooly, editor,
Information Week

Extranets

The foundation of any business-to-business system is your extranet. This will give you the channel to create secure communications between your intranet, and shared portions of the system that are externalized to the business partner(s). Hence the term *extranet.*

The extranet provides a secure gateway for visitors coming in from outside the organization, and gives them controlled access to the portions of data that they have permission to see, modify or publish. In some cases, the extranet can also be used to provide access to internal systems via a Web interface, or through some other means (PDA, voice browser etc.). This allows business partners to gain access not just to data that is located on the extranet Web, but other internal systems that are important to the business relationship.

Most applications can be delivered via an extranet, and most extranets are secure at the application level. This means that the business partner submits a password to gain access to the system (obviously, other security schemes can be used, but this is a common one).

In addition to electronic mail and secure posting of information some starter applications for an extranet include the following (Table 5.1).

Table 5.1 Sample starter applications for a business-to-business extranet.

Technology	Application
Secure electronic mail	Business-to-business communications
Bulletin board	Subject review and response vehicle, frequently asked questions
Instant messaging	Sales and Customer support
Document Repository	Knowledge Management and customer support
FTP	Customer support, sales support, software development
Mail list server	Broadcast of changes and notifications
Calendar	Scheduling
Data conferencing and chat	Electronic meetings
Voice over IP	Information delivery to cell and land lines, PDAs

While these may be typical for your first extranet applications there are no limits to how sophisticated your extranet could become. As you consider the development of your extranet, you must regard security as the number one concern. Visitors coming into the extranet usually deal with sensitive data that is confidential in nature. Also, ensure that external business partners have access only to information appropriate for your specific business arrangement.

> **VIRTUAL PRIVATE NETWORKS**
>
> Private networks that allow users to purchase bandwidth and access, often through their Internet connection, without them needing to purchase dedicated network cabling or systems.

Smart
things
to know

Until recently, it was difficult to consider creating an extranet without first having an intranet, however this has changed. Since 1999, new extranet solutions have emerged that are hosted outside of the company facilities. (These are hosted by Application Service Providers.) If you want to develop an extranet, but don't want your staff to bear the everyday burden of administration and support, this is a reasonable alternative. This way you have the benefit of avoiding buying sophisticated security software, as the hosting firm offering the system will provide the majority of the security tools. However, the net effect is the same for the extranet systems' users.

Virtual Private Networks

Virtual private networks (VPNs) are another popular method of providing point-to-point security for business-to-business networks. By using a VPN you and your partners' businesses can connect in a secure manner, but still have the convenience of the Internet as the wire to transmit the data. This can save thousands of dollars, and allows easy access for your partners who need to collaborate with you.

Virtual private networks have become the most common method of linking remote offices to a common network. The technology used to make this happen is known as *tunneling*. As the name suggests, it provides a way of linking various VPN locations across the Internet while enforcing security.

Many large telecommunication companies in the market are re-marketing their excess capacity to VPN providers. You may find this a good method to acquire additional bandwidth without the need to pay until you use it. As each month passes, new technology is becoming more affordable. Depending where your business is located, this technology will impact the choice of network. By using a combination of a VPN for a group of suppliers, and then delivering applications that can meet their needs, the concept of a ready-made extranet has become a reality.

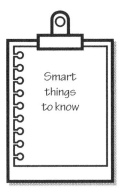

Smart
things
to know

TUNNELING

A secure mechanism to allow transmission of data across points of access on the Internet.

You can select software and hosting firms who offer packages that allow groups of businesses to collaborate using ready-made applications from day one. Most of these applications require a sign-up process on the Internet and then you are ready to go. You can expect many more of these in the coming months and years.

VPNs are a particularly good choice if you are considering supply-chain applications, where you need to be connected to a partners network for a longer period, or may need access to multiple applications outside the scope of a simpler collaborative extranet.

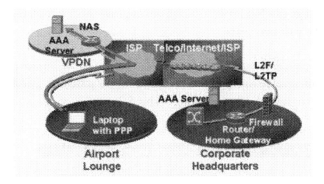

Fig. 5.2 Virtual private networks example. Courtesy Cisco Systems.

Supply chains

Supply chains are a well-established method of linking businesses and their processes together. Many are focused on building, selling and supporting products in national and multinational chains.

Companies who have successful supply-chain and manufacturing systems put themselves ahead of others in the market. Creating this advantage and staying flexible to meet differing market conditions gives these leading companies an edge that is hard to beat.

Firms such as Dell Computer, who have combined their focus on the end customer with a great Web delivery strategy, have gone from strength to strength. They build all their products to order, and are currently accumulating these orders to the value of more than $50 million daily from their e-business Web site. At the other end of the spectrum Boeing, a leading producer of capital goods, has invested heavily to improve its supply-chain organization in the past two years.

Businesses use supply-chain management software and systems to improve the way their businesses are operating. Typical reasons for purchasing and implementing systems include the following (Table 5.2).

Table 5.2 Reasons for supply-chain management systems.

Function	Desired improvement
Inventory management	Cut inventory volume
Manufacturing management	Ensure that products are delivered on time in most efficient manner
	Cut manufacturing cycle times
	Increase revenues
Procurement	Reduction in costs of goods produced
Distribution management	Improved sales and delivery timeframes

Smart things to say

The Internet is influencing the behavior of supply-chain systems and provides a tremendous opportunity for companies to leverage their strengths in ways not possible before.

As more firms' products and services continue to expand at a global level, the need to consider the impact of the Internet and supply-chain systems increases. The cost of entering sophisticated supply chains and systems is changing.

The Internet is influencing the behavior of supply-chain systems and providing a tremendous opportunity for companies to leverage their strengths in ways not possible before. Companies such as L.L. Bean and Lands End offer products directly on their Web site, even offering consumers the ability to configure products directly in the Web environment. The computer industry has done a great job also in this space.

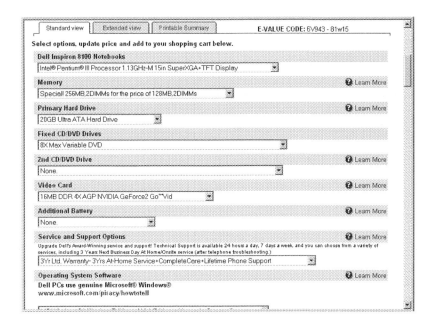

Fig. 5.3 Dell Computer's on-line store with direct access to configuration management system for end users.

Businesses use supply chains to improve their competitive position in the marketplace. Management continues to concern itself with the issues of globalization, competition and meeting the demands of consumers. These come high on the list of driving reasons to continue to develop the supply chain and hone its operation. Many companies in the past have focused on various individual aspects of the problem, such as procurement or inventory management. Today the view tends to be much more holistic, with a total review of parties involved in all aspects of the supply chain to create the best potential value and results.

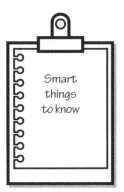

REASONS FOR SUPPLY-CHAIN MANAGEMENT

The benefits of supply-chain management include:

- consumer and business demand for improved service, more choice and lower costs;
- competition is increasing all the time;
- more parts and finished goods may have to be shipped to different locations around the world; and
- Internet and related technologies have a potentiallly huge impact on the rate of change in distribution supply chains and consumer behavior.

The Internet has created some significant opportunities for companies to create a virtual supply chain of partners inside their current markets as well as outside. This allows firms to more rapidly develop the support mechanisms and systems to build clear improvements in the way that they are operating in the marketplace.

By using existing supply-chain software, and systems that are already in place in the organization, companies can add significant value to their product offerings.

Smart quotes

Referring to Philips' aim to have its entire base of 1000 distributors on-line:

"By then, you'll do business with us electronically, or you won't do business with us."

Jim Worth, director of e-business at Philips Lighting Co.

Business-to-business exchanges

There are three primary types of B2B business exchanges now operating in the market. These are the private exchanges, procurement marketplaces and industry-specific exchanges.

Each of these sites offers a specific set of benefits for members and participants. The recent meltdown of exchanges in the industry that do not offer significant value has thinned the ranks to the fittest and ones providing most value. Their goals are now simple: to provide efficiency and a better way of doing business for the members of the exchange. Whether private, procurement-specific or industry-specific, the components of each of these systems is the same (Table 5.3).

Table 5.3 B2B components and the support they provide to business exchanges and marketplaces.

B2B components of a system	Function
Business rules	How business is done
Processes	Protocols and support for the process
Technology (and transaction support)	Underlying systems to support the business function combined with the technology to encapsulate the rules and processes

Each business-to-business system should provide value by connecting partners in an improved supply chain for either product or service. Elements of each of these areas are often broken down into smaller parts, allowing use of components or partial solutions in divisions of a company's operation.

B2B exchanges and marketplace, and their participants, create either performance improvement for their members, or "interference" for existing players in a supply chain. Sometimes the creation of the marketplace is based on knowledge of an opportunity where "inefficiency" is inherent, and therein lies the potential to improve or remove it. Sometimes, this is as simple as "too many in the food chain" where a Web-based system can improve things quickly, and remove unneeded members. However, most systems today need to add more value than purely cutting steps out of the process. Successful exchanges, such as Altera, (a US-based energy marketplace), are based on enterprises that have a great deal of skills experience in, and focus on, one particular vertical market. This knowledge then provides the basis for the new and improved business model.

An important principal to grasp with any B2B system is that they do not stand alone. While vendors and analysts continue to "categorize" technologies, sometimes for good reason, it creates a huge confusion factor for managers and buyers out there trying to figure out what is going on. As Fig. 5.4 illustrates, it is possible to have many different types of B2B systems involved in a single company or operation. It is crucial to understand this

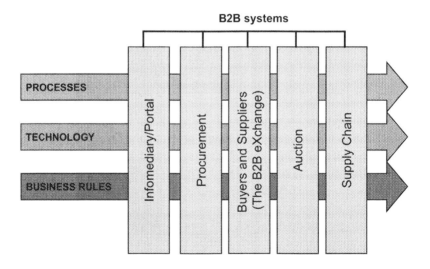

Fig. 5.4 Components in a B2B marketplace. Courtesy: Perseus Books, *B2B: How to Build a Profitable E-Commerce Strategy*, Michael J. Cunningham.

multi-dimensional aspect, whether you are selecting or developing a B2B strategy.

Digital markets – procurement

The procurement marketplace was one of the earliest to be adopted by many in their e-commerce programs. Vendors and suppliers in this market saw advantages to be gained in sharing information and prices for products and services that were required for internal needs. The obvious benefits of B2B systems such as these include avoiding the creation of complex approval cycles for minor items. The paperwork required for purchasing small office supplies, for instance, costs more than the items themselves.

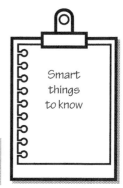

Smart things to know

> B2B systems include portals, procurement, exchanges and supply-chain systems.

These benefits notwithstanding, automating and enforcing business rules for the purchase of a wide range of systems soon became the focus for procurement systems. In particular, the automation of B2B applications where there are many suppliers and components has resulted in significant benefits, including:

- reduced costs of items in the procurement market;

- improved availability;

- ability to reduce inventory for buyers;

- controlled procurement processes;

- ability to control quality standards more effectively;

- improved cash management; and

- supplier control expansion and improvement.

These systems are now forming the heart of many supply-chain systems, but can also be much simpler in nature. E-procurement decisions can now be made directly from the buyers' organizations, on-line through their intranets and B2E (business to employee) systems. Some of these are through links, and others are a sublicensed component of the digital market itself. As an example, Staples and Travelocity.com are suppliers of digital procurement services that businesses can use by ordering on-line. The large procurement systems – such as those used by the State of California to improve their e-government initiatives – are often the ones that steal the headlines. However, the market is expanding with simple applications that meet many B2B internal requirements. The examples in Table 5.4 show how e-procurement systems can deal with headaches for small and medium-size businesses today:

Table 5.4 Some e-procurement solutions.

Business issue	B2B procurement solution
Corporate travel	On-line travel agency
Hardware and software acquisition	Hardware and software supplier with configuration control
Payroll and 401k	On-line payroll services, retirement management services
Banking	On-line banking and accounting services
Shipping	On-line shipping services

These are all useful B2B market services. Many of these are outgrowths of existing on-line services that have provided outsourcing of either product or services in the recent years. Outsourcing payroll has been a long-time service provided by firms such as Ceridian and ADP. However, moving on-line can allow the client to provide self-service functions for many of these operations, allowing the client more flexibility, while reducing the support costs for the system.

E-MARKETPLACES

The exchange is a place where suppliers, buyers and intermediaries can congregate and offer products to each other with a predefined set of business rules to conduct the transaction.

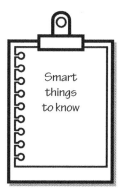

Smart
things
to know

Many of these activities make great sense, as many of these services were too expensive to offer when the bulk of the transaction needed human interaction. Once the business rules are electronically applied, there is little need for significant human intervention. Shipping and billing information is often created automatically; in some cases, accounts are settled on-line using digital cash or credits.

The range of these services is continuing to expand. However, many operations are learning that the savings apply only if they work well for the client. Customer service to support these activities still requires some level of "escalation" and "human touch" to ensure that problems are resolved rapidly. Organizations such as CitiGroup intend to dramatically grow these services by becoming a one-stop shopping location for B2B applications. A powerful combination of payroll, shipping, office equipment, credit services, travel, e-commerce, investment and insurance services, makes for an interesting set of business functions centralized around a single procurement system. The value of these services is becoming self-evident, as e-procurement takes its rightful place high on the list of B2B applications.

Digital markets – the B2B exchange

Independent of the procurement marketplace is the now well-established marketplace known as the B2B exchange. This exchange is a place where suppliers, buyers and intermediaries can congregate and offer products to each other with a predefined set of business rules to conduct the transaction. The newest of all B2B models, it has been the one causing the most consternation. Despite many cries of disintermediation in the business-to-consumer market, it seems that they shouted too early from the hilltops. In the business-to-consumer market, it took some time for intermediaries to enter the market, but when they did, they provided valuable services for consumers looking for products on the Web. Comparison-shopping Web sites and supporting review sites have become very popular. So does that mean that all the shouting was for naught? Perhaps, perhaps not.

Before, the Internet was a commonplace vehicle for commerce. Many organizations had their operations and margins affected as others made changes to the B2B value chain they were in. The computer industry is a good example, where hardware and software moved through huge distributors like TechData. These suppliers provided a valuable service to the market, but at the same time caused the margins of many products to drop from highs gained by smaller companies in the distribution channel. This resulted in changes in distribution strategies for those vendors previously in the channel. Were they disintermediated? Yes, and with good reason: they were not adding enough value in the chain.

One main difference with B2B is that the value chain changes rapidly, particularly in a digital market where the development of new rules makes it easy for others to participate. Operations such as GoFish.com are good examples of where a new marketplace provides considerable value to those involved in the process (Fig. 5.5).

The concept for this operation was born on the waterfront of Maine's fishing industry, to provide a single location for buyers and sellers in the fishing industry. GoFish management developed some powerful differentiators to make it hard for competitors to "mussel in" on their territory. The seafood industry was characterized by fragmented communications and a situation where "buying critical" information was difficult to obtain. By linking buyers and sellers along with relevant information in real time, GoFish has developed a considerable niche.

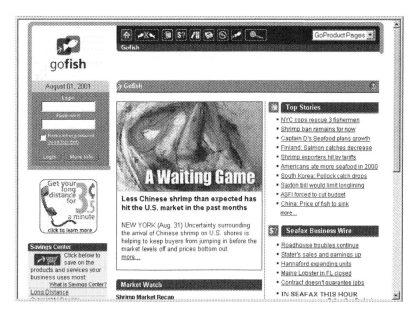

Fig. 5.5 GoFish.com – an industry exchange focused on the seafood industry.

Another major issue in the seafood industry was the creditworthiness of buyers. With a sales background with Dunn & Bradstreet, GoFish founder Niel Workman rapidly recognized the value of credit information in a market with a "product that had to be sold quickly," and long receivable cycles. In addition to putting this information on-line, GoFish created a partnership to resolve the receivable problem for the fisherman. By guaranteeing payment to the seller, typically within 48 hours, much of the bad-debt risk has been removed from the market – at least from qualified suppliers and buyers in the GoFish network. Creating a sophisticated and valuable service is establishing the firm as a leader with a sustainable position in the marketplace. A financial partnership with GE Capital provides the equivalent of short-term banking services to their client base.

Each of the players contributes something to the digital marketplace. Each digital marketplace can vary considerably, some will be closed to many, others will be available only by invitation, and others will be open to a wide range of players. Digital marketplaces operate based on rules that are defined by the owner or by the participants' rules (if this option is permitted by the host). The host of the marketplace usually understands a particular market sector well, and then determines how to offer services to its members. In many cases these exchanges are operating today more as sophisticated portals and infomediaries, connecting buyers, traders, sellers and intermediaries utilizing content to build the traffic and credibility of the site. In some cases these relationships can be as simple as a vendor/supplier relationship, or more complex as illustrated in Fig. 5.6.

Exchanges are predicated on changing the way that supply networks operate. Many want to participate and do so based on a percentage of the transaction fee, but others work on a subscription or other membership basis. Some companies have started out with a strategy to build business partnerships in volume, at attractive fees to their clients, then as the market starts to evolve, the business model changes. Suddenly, participants are expected

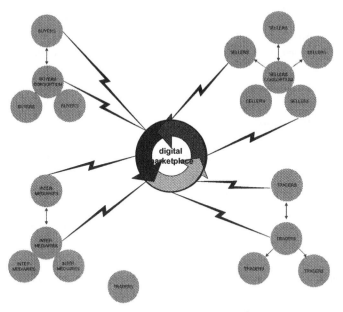

Fig. 5.6 Players in a digital marketplace.

Table 5.5 Examples of different business models for exchange membership and revenue.

Business model	Transaction type
Membership or subscription	Fixed annual fee, or usage subscription base
Percentage of transaction	Share of transaction, based on pre-agreed business model
Referral fee	Percentage on agreed-fee basis
Auction	Based on auction rules for buyers and sellers of products in the exchange
Purchase of products/service	Based on transaction rules determined before entering and participating in the exchange

to pay large commission payments, and the lucrative contracts are funneled to exchange members willing to pay the fees. Whether you are a user or plan to build a business exchange, there are myriad methods and reasons to participate.

The portal and the infomediary

Both of these terms are often misused and misinterpreted today. In literal terms the word "portal" literally means a gateway. Therefore, a portal in the Internet world provides an "entrance" into something. Portals started out as transitory sites such as search engines, as it was (and still is) difficult to find where to start in the search for relevant information on the Web. These portal sites grew from pure indexes into information centers providing news, views and relevant information for the user. This content progression was intended to keep the user on the site longer, which resulted in more pages viewed, and more advertising generated. Other sites used the Web as a means to present and sell information – often publishing companies amortizing their investment in content along with a desire to create a more valuable business proposition for their investors and clients alike. The infomediary was born, and now services many organizations with information relevant to their topical desires.

Another factor development that impacts the B2B world is the self created portal – or the intranet. The intranet is the "home base" of the portal world. As the company or organization develops the intranet, it is usually packed with germane information designed to improve the productivity and information flow in the internal operation. We will examine some dramatic examples of how to use intranets for B2B applications later in the book. A good place for organizations to start with the development of their own portal is at the intranet, particularly for functions and applications closely tied to the desktop of the operation. Intranet functions that go beyond internal company usage include extranets and virtual private networks for working closely and interacting with business partners and suppliers.

In business-to-business terms, the portal is usually a one-stop destination, specific to an individual industry or function in the B2B cycle. These portals can have a very wide range of focus.

The auction

The auction model can be used in many different B2B systems, and is not exclusive to particular participants.

We are discussing the auction as a separate model in the B2B world, mainly because it has some unique characteristics that are different from the others involved in this process. However, it should be clear that the auctions model can be used anywhere in these models in many different ways. There is nothing to stop an individual company from including auction functionality from both the sale and buy side of their B2B transaction.

The auction model, is often considered a more open method of trading. Many existing business-to-consumer sites offer very simplified auctions rules and systems to allow buyers and sellers to come together in a common market. This allows inventory to be created without buying it, and fulfillment to occur, often without any payment transaction being managed by the site.

Examples are the easiest way to describe complex systems, and the auction is no exception. If you were to participate in a typical B2B auction site for hardware and software systems, you might visit a site such as Egghead/ Onsale. The procedure would go something like this:

1   You register yourself (or company) with the auction company along with the appropriate credit card information and shipping preferences.

2   During the registration process you will be asked to review and sign up to on-line agreements that outline the rules of purchases from their site. They will also outline the rules that apply in the auction, and the various categories of products available for the auction.

3   Additional tools such as automated bidding and monitoring tools will be included in this review process. Most auction systems have some form of these tools, this avoids you having to continuously return to the site to review how your bid is doing. Notices are distributed via email or instant messaging alerts to your desktop.

4   Once registered and in agreement with the business rules, you are ready to participate.

5   Most auctions have the variables of time, price and volume as the major components. Each participant enters a bid (sometimes with an upper limit if the site has an automated bidding tool), and then watches for what will happen next.

6   If the auction site is providing all of the components, and you are successful, the site will email you shipping details and the price at which the product or service was procured. Usually they will debit your account for this amount.

7   Disputes are usually handled by automated customer support tools. If the dispute is significant then you can get on the phone to them to resolve the problem.

The auction

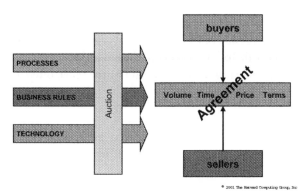

Fig. 5.7 The auction. Courtesy: Perseus Books, *B2B: How to Build a Profitable E-Commerce Strategy*, Michael J. Cunningham.

8 The auction business rules are very important to you if you decide to offer these facilities on your B2B site. Ensuring that you are assigning business rules that are acceptable in your individual market or product area is a key to success in a suitable model. There is also the opportunity of using other auction models and facilities. This can dramatically reduce the costs and efforts associated with this model option.

The reverse auction

Another interesting twist on the auction model is the reverse auction. This is the same as a buying auction, but in reverse. Here companies that have services and products that are in-demand place themselves in a reverse auction where others can bid to provide them. These are becoming increasingly popular and are changing our perceptions of supplier-buyer-supplier relationships.

One reason for this is that the reverse auction allows potential buyers to "comparison-shop" without any commitment until they see the options available to them. Many sites are starting to incorporate the reverse auction to provide value to both buyers and sellers, and to create a location for new relationships to be established. Today, in general, the buyer does not pay a fee to participate (or shop); most of the fees are paid by the seller, often as a success fee.

The supply chain

The use of business-to-business strategies to support company operations is not a new phenomenon. Industries have been using business-to-business strategies and processes to support the development of their products, services and partnerships for many years. For example, the aerospace industry has been working with partners in the airframe, avionics and engine categories. All of these are members of supply-chain groups who co-ordinate design, development, testing, acceptance, production and maintenance of products and systems.

Other industries are moving rapidly into the adoption of supply-chain business-to-business systems. All the major automotive firms now have a huge supply-chain program in place.

All of these are designed to improve the efficiency of their businesses and the way they deal with partners in the development, manufacturing, support and sales cycles. These systems allow contributors in the supply chain to view status information for inventory, orders and deliveries within the framework of the production process.

Before the Internet, the benefits of supply-chain management were considered high enough to invest in specialized networks and infrastructure to link members of the chain together. The Internet now allows us to connect these groups in a common system at a much-reduced cost, and the need for sophisticated and expensive communication systems is negated. Today, with the Internet in place, the cost of building these systems is much lower, making it much easier and cost-effective to extend them.

As many firms have already made the necessary investment to create these interdependent relationships with suppliers and business partners, the Web offers a unique opportunity to further extend and improve these systems.

Companies with existing supply chains understand the power and relevance of these systems. Companies like Dell Computer have united an end-user focus with a superb Web-delivery system. This has worked remarkably well for them, to the point that most of their business is created from on-line orders. Dell builds new products directly from customers' orders, thereby limiting expensive inventory costs and making it easier for them to upgrade and change with technology improvements. Today they are taking orders for more than $50 million worth of products on-line though their B2B and B2C site. Companies use supply-management systems for many reasons, including:

- reducing manufacturing cycle times;

- reducing product development, production and manufacturing cycles;

- improved sales and delivery timeframes;

- reducing inventory;

- increasing revenues; and

- reducing costs of goods.

A wide range of existing supply-chain software and systems is in the process of being converted to meet Web-based and browser standards, so these systems can be extended easily to meet a variety of market trends.

Business networks and syndication

Development of a business network for e-business is still an evolving concept. Business networks differ from supply-chain networks in several ways.

Supply-chain networks usually involve manufacturing products and, much less so, services; business networks can include both. Business networks often involve direct distribution channels but can also involve other partners that have relative value for the overall function or market area of activity.

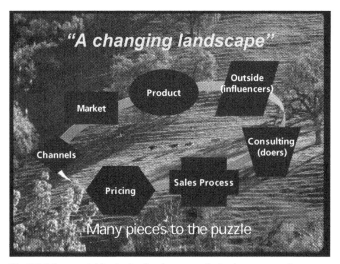

Fig. 5.8 Many variables in the development of a business network.

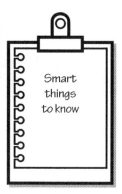

CHANNELS

Distribution channels to provide alternative ways of selling and supporting product instead of selling direct to the consumer.

For the successful development of any business network, all aspects of the sales, distribution and support process have to be considered. In order to ensure that there is effective distribution of the product or service, it should meet the requirements of the market, the distribution channels and users/consumers of the products.

One useful way to consider these is to visualize the variables in the framework of a distributed ecosystem. As with other ecosystems, plants survive in the ones that provide the best support for them. When it moves out of the ecosystem, the results change and the outcome is different. When developing a business network these variables need to be carefully considered and also how the product will be priced, packaged, distributed, delivered and supported, based on the end-user needs and market conditions. Developing programs that support these types of networks needs careful thinking, and smart moves. By using other channels, the cost of creating effective distribution can be lowered, and the risk associated with a single-channel initiative reduced.

One method of building and expanding a business network is to create a group of affiliate organizations. If you have a product that can be sold by others, some dramatic options are available to increase channel bandwidth and effectiveness.

Amazon.com has created a vast business network of affiliates by offering associates part of their profit margin resulting from sales or referrals. This type of business network and syndication of products is a very inventive method to gain improved market visibility.

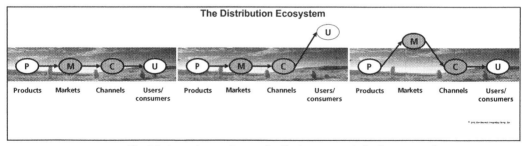

Fig. 5.9 Areas that can impact distribution strategy in business networks.

Fig. 5.10 The Amazon.com associates program allows others to sell their products.

As companies' distribution needs increase, along with the requirement to customize content through a business-to-business network, the obvious next stage for development of the market is syndication of product and content. This next stage of the market is about to explode, with products, technology and new distribution strategies that are likely to make jaws drop even amongst the more skeptical.

Syndication

This next phenomenon will allow companies to quickly and easily create their own business networks, complete with management tools for the affiliates and others in the chain of distribution. The technology that will allow this to occur is called XML. XML is a new way of describing data in the Internet space, one that allows companies to define their own language and protocols in their business networks. It has already been in successful deployment for over 18 months, but has been supported in standard browser technology only since the release of version 5.0 browsers from Microsoft and Netscape.

Syndication is likely to be successful because it allows the same product to be presented differently, packaged differently, and priced differently to targeted audiences. It will also allow for the reuse of content on a major scale, without all of the technical indigestion and work of the early years in Web development.

By proactively managing affiliates, it will become easy to ensure that you can offer your brand and products to as many Web sites as possible, at the same time actually reducing the amount of work involved in the process. The technology currently on the market to support these functions will allow customized management of content and digital delivery of only the relevant content for that particular member of the business network.

Syndication

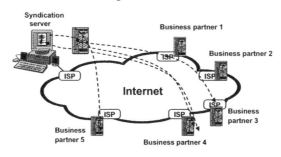

©1999 The Harvard Computing Group, Inc.

Fig. 5.11 Syndicated content and information being distributed to business partners.

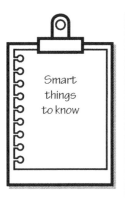

Smart
things
to know

SYNDICATION

- Syndicate when you have components that can be used in many different assembly and product configurations.
- Syndicate when you have a product that many people want, but your business partners want to brand it themselves.
- Syndicate when you want to get your products or services located on as many affiliate Web sites as possible.
- Syndicate if you have content that can be re-purposed in many ways.
- Syndicate if you have an e-business offering that will add value to others in your business network.

Making them work

Organizations around the globe are using Internet business-to-business technologies in truly productive and astounding ways. These range from procurement systems that automate the way that materials and products are purchased, through to the most sophisticated customer management systems to improve and automate the process.

The categories of systems in the market for business-to-business e-business cover a wide range. After all, is the customer management system that is sitting in the corner of the data center providing just as much value as another that is processing orders? For many applications we tend to consider only the money-collecting aspect of these systems. However, any productivity improvements that drop to the bottom line are considered fair game for e-business applications.

Smart quotes

"There has to be an executive sponsor from the top that has the e-business religion. If that person isn't up there saying that the Web is one of the most important things in our business today, you're simply not going to move fast enough."

Phil Gibson, director of Interactive Marketing at National Semiconductor

Customer management systems

The customer management example is a great way to consider how to really leverage e-business solutions. With the continuing expense and shortage of qualified IT staff in the US market, many firms are focusing on knowledge bases and customer management systems that are Internet based to pick up the shortfall.

One such firm, which recognized the staffing problem early in their development, was Cisco Systems. They started out early in this process to build a Web site that would provide the information that their clients were looking for, particularly related to their software products and support. This consisted of providing software updates in downloadable form, with the accompanying documentation, all available via the Internet. Cisco estimates that they have saved themselves over $75 million in staff costs alone, along with the packaging and shipping savings resulting from most of the software products being downloaded from the Web. In 1998, they estimated these savings alone to be in the order of $250 million. Today, the Web deals with more than 70% of their support calls, without additional intervention required. Technology firms such as Transitions Systems, Inc. have also benefited from e-business solutions based on linking knowledge bases to customer databases. In a bold move this software company made the decision to develop their knowledge management repository for their clients and business partners, and at the same time implement an enterprise customer relationship management system.

While initially they had considered implementing just one of these systems, the dramatic difference in the return on investment from the combination made them make the bold move.

Smart things to think about

- Use customer management systems to assist in the delivery and recording of business-to-business transactions.
- Create knowledge bases that will allow business partners to get access to information via your extranet.

Using the intranet as a foundation for business-to-business

Intranets are a major component of e-business strategies. These systems evolve from many starting points – from strategic initiatives with departmental or enterprise support to opportunities based on speed and cost constraints. Intranets have created a need to integrate content, maintain performance, share information, control access, and deal with other intranets. Multiple intranet servers, connected by local and wide area networks (LANs and WANs), provide the foundation for distributed intranets.

REASONS TO CONSIDER INTRANETS IN BUSINESS-TO-BUSINESS
APPLICATIONS

- Intranets provide organizations with a flexible way to organize information that can be shared with others in a controlled and expandable way.
- Companies such as MCI WorldCom are using large-scale, distributed intranets to help newly acquired companies become integrated into their operations in months, not years. Distributed intranets can help companies like MCI WorldCom receive a return on their technology investment as high as 500–2000%.
- An intranet's technology components are now the raw materials of almost every desktop, and support the lowest common denominator of IT standards – the browser, HTTP, and TCP/IP. Nothing on that list scares even the most conservative of IT staffers.

Smart things to think about

Today, most organizations no longer view intranets as a separate component of their IT strategy, and have moved towards a flexible way of organizing information where the content can be shared with others in a controlled, expandable way. This philosophy provides the foundation for the development of distributed intranets. Also, as intranets become richer in content, and this content is extended to partners and customers, extranets are born. From the architectural point of view, the extranet is merely a protected section of the intranet.

Many firms develop intranets to improve productivity and increase the speed with which information is delivered to their organization. In environments that have a great need to provide accurate information in timely fashion, an intranet and its natural ability to expand has made it the technology choice. Intranets often provide the basis for the delivery of information needed by the internal staff, such as an employee telephone directory, human resource policies, support information, and a knowledge base. Extranet access can also be offered for some intranet-based information, such as support information and the knowledge base.

Citigroup has 300,000 US customers banking on-line with 25,000 being added each week.

Ed Horowitz, a senior corporate officer at Citigroup, says it costs Citigroup $450 a year to service a customer in a bricks-and-mortar branch compared with less than $150 on the Web.

Business needs have been vital to the rapid development of intranets. Typical business drivers include the need to rapidly adapt to change, to distribute information, and show dissatisfaction with existing information-delivery techniques. Other factors include supporting major strategic initiatives such as knowledge management, e-business, or customer relationship management. Typical business and productivity drivers for intranet solutions include:

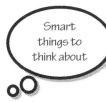

REASONS TO DEPLOY INTRANETS

- *Employee productivity.* Dynamic information, shorter cycle times, and increased accuracy.
- *Cost savings.* On-line information distribution versus paper and lower maintenance costs.
- *Knowledge management.* KM lets you customize information to meet users' needs.
- *E-business.* E-business typically means customized content, presentation, and transactions.
- *Customer management improvements.* Integrating business processes with customer relationship management and client-specific information improves business cycles.

Intranets are also a low-cost technology and, on top of that, they scale. For example, MCI WorldCom's intranet chief architect, Kevin Crothers, moved his company intranet from 20,000 to 100,000 users in less than two years. He estimates that MCI WorldCom has used only a fraction of its intranet system capacity, although the company is currently averaging 1.5 million hits per hour with peaks of up to 12 million. (MCI WorldCom has an actively logged-on community of 45,000 to 50,000 users.)

Crothers says that MCI WorldCom relies on intranet technology to ensure that newly acquired companies are integrated into the operation in months, not years. MCI WorldCom's distributed network includes 500 intranet sites (150 of which are linked under a universal server), 120 IP networks, 1000 servers, and 70,000 workstations serving roughly 55,000 employees. The staff to develop, deploy, and maintain this large-scale distributed intranet includes 105 staff members and contractors.

Employees browse the intranet using either a Microsoft Internet Explorer or Netscape Navigator browser. Intranet applications include an interactive intranet for facilitating IT communications and intranet collaboration, and a Web forum designed to bring together business groups from across the company to analyze how to leverage critical technology tools. Over 600 people from six different sites dialed in to the first real-time collaboration venture, saving the company thousands of dollars in travel costs and downtime.

MCI WorldCom also launched www.wcom.com, an extranet that lets customers access the company's internal customer service information to review their current service and sign up for new programs and services.

While many organizations might not be able to match such an aggressive pace, there are still barriers you need to surpass before you can install an intranet and expect automatic productivity improvements. Many of these are associated with culture and work process change. For example, if your company emphasizes rewards for individual efforts, employees may resist team-building and team-oriented initiatives. If you have a hierarchical management structure, individuals may find it hard to adjust to collaborative teams. Failure to understand and address issues like these ultimately influences your organization's success. Much of an intranet's productivity gains are based on effective behavioral change in the enterprise, so it's critical to ensure that corporate culture and processes change, by linking these to the system. MCI WorldCom estimates that it has saved more than $45 million in publication costs, employee productivity, and reduced maintenance and development costs since deploying an intranet. For many organizations such as this, the intranet has become a strategic business tool, not just a "nice-to-have" technology option.

The speed and timing of such changes are also important in developing and delivering new work practices. In the large scale, distributed systems

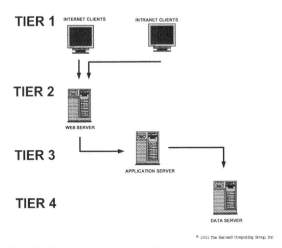

© 2001 The Harvard Computing Group, Inc

Fig. 5.12 Example of an n-tier architecture.

at MCI WorldCom, bringing new employees into the newly merged entity happened with incredible speed. One business day after the merger between MCI and WorldCom, the corporate intranet grew from 22,000 to 110,000 users. All 110,000 users had password access to the enlarged system.

Supply-chain management

A powerful example of leveraging supply-chain management is Cisco Systems. As a global supplier, Cisco has manufacturing plants in many countries. Managing this network of plants, suppliers, business partners is critical to the firm. Their supply-chain system supported by a powerful e-business system has made a huge impact on their bottom line. In their annual report for 1998, the company reports savings totaling $500 million because of these systems.

Smart things to know

> Cisco Systems saved $1.5 billion last year through increased operational efficiency and cost avoidance.

Cisco has used configuration management and on-line ordering systems since 1997. These tools help their business partners select and configure, get pricing information and conduct business-to-business e-business. Cisco has been the poster child for operations using the Internet for internal and business partner efficiency. The firm claims to have saved $1.5 billion in 2000 through increased operational efficiency and cost avoidance. With business-to-business sales of more than $19 billion in 2000, Cisco represents one of the largest firms of e-business in industry today.

Internet commerce

Many business-to-business applications continue to develop in the market-place. Table 5.6 illustrates how some firms have used business-to-business to better improve their position in the marketplace, and enhance their business.

Table 5.6 Improving market position through B2B.

Industry	Applications	Example
Banking	On-line banking	BankBoston
High tech manufacturing	Supply-chain management	Cisco Systems
Insurance	Policy applications	Intuit
High tech wholesalers and retailers	Procurement and auctions	Egghead.com
Education	Distance learning	NTU
Clothing and retail	Configuration management and e-business	Lands' End
Telecommunications	Video-conferencing	A T & T
Publishing	Business-to-business content, newsfeeds	Ziff Davis (zdnet.com)
Stock market	Stock trading	Charles Schwab

The future

Business-to-business activities remain the largest sector of the market, and show no signs of stopping. As companies start to really understand the power of the Internet, and combine the technology with integrated business strategies, powerful results will emerge. There is almost no limit to where the future might take us in this direction. Certainly the businesses that have an existing brand name and the ability to leverage their existing supply chains and relationships may have an advantage – but only if they use it.

Many of the new business-to-business solutions have been made successful by creating a new offering that the "traditional" business has either ignored, or been scared to go into uncharted territory. Even the large, aircraft-carrier-size companies can be turned around when there is a desire to do so. Just look at IBM's revival in fortune since Mr Gerstner's arrival.

Whether your focus is going to be business-to-consumer, or business-to-business both will be relevant to making your organization work better. Even if you just take advantage of the business-to-business services out there in the marketplace, to help you cut procurement costs and improve information access and flow inside the organization.

6

Building Your Own Strategy

ON HOW AN E-BUSINESS STRATEGY CAN INFLUENCE A BUSINESS

"I am often asked how the Internet has changed our business at Charles Schwab. The perhaps surprising answer is: 'It really hasn't.' Rather than fundamentally changing our business, the Internet has *enhanced* the way we have been operating since I founded the company back in 1971."

Charles R. Schwab, founder and chairman, The Charles Schwab Corporation

Smart things to think about

The above quote from Charles Schwab might seem a little conservative on first reading. However, when you see how Schwab have used technology to *enhance* their business it has been focused, dramatic, and shows tremendous market leadership. Schwab's drive as a business leader has fostered an environment that demands excellence and continuous concern about competitors.

For us mortals out there, understanding how and where to start developing our business strategy for e-business often causes consternation, not just new opportunities. As earlier chapters illustrate, just understanding the basics can be a task in itself. Determining why you need a strategy in the first place is a critical starting point (Table 6.1).

Table 6.1 Some of the reasons for the development of a strategy.

Positive reasons	Negative reasons
Expand the business	Pressure from competition
Improve marketing	Concern about adoption
Increase competitiveness	Decreasing market share
Desire to take leadership position	Worry

Surprisingly, many firms developed their strategies because of concern about their market position. This worry factor is often high, and while we may not know what to do, we do know we have to do something. Some organizations have developed their strategies with external help, others spend months meandering around the problem, and approach the task in a piecemeal manner.

Development of any strategy often involves complex decisions and changes in the organization, but finding where to go first has some simple principles.

Smart answers to tough questions

Q: I know that I need do something about e-business, but where do I start?

A: Start by looking for the most important reasons (both positive and negative) in the organization why you should develop a strategy. Ask yourself and some close colleagues if you think that the organization would support an e-business strategy if they could successfully deal with these issues. Try looking for the leading questions and challenges facing you today.

Most of these factors revolve around money. Creating more revenue, reducing costs, improving margins and becoming more competitive. However, not all organizations using e-business are linked tightly around pure return on investment. Government and other not-for-profit organizations may be driven by goals such as:

- improving lifestyles;

- philanthropy;

- reducing administration;

- improving research and results; and

- supporting their staff and volunteers more effectively.

Types of strategy – your appetite for change

Understanding your organization's appetite for change is a major influence in the development of your strategy. Most organizations have a very variable appetite for change. These range from the voracious to the staid. Determining where you fit into this pattern also determines how fast and dramatically you can act.

Certain factors surrounding you determine how much change is acceptable to an organization. Bill Gates, (chairman of Microsoft Corporation) is an example of someone who, once committed to the Internet, caused his aircraft-carrier-size organization to change and change quickly. Most managers do not have the capability (or resources) to cause such rapid change to occur.

E-business has a lot in common with other high-impact strategies; too little change can have virtually no impact on the outcome, too much can risk the fundamentals of the business. As most organizations implement change incrementally, determining the acceptable levels and risk factors influences your strategy development. Table 6.2 illustrates examples where differing amounts of change affect the development of an organization's e-business strategy.

Table 6.2 Illustration of differing appetites for e-business change in the organization.

Organization size	Age	Competitiveness in marketplace	Financial strength	Regulated for change	Appetite
>1000 staff	10	Strong	Strong	No	Medium to low
>1000 staff medium	10	Low	Low	No	High to
>1000 staff	10	Strong	Strong	Yes	Low
~20 staff	1–2	Moderate	Moderate	No	Very high
~20 staff	10	Good	Good	No	Medium

Factors such as regulation, the internal culture, how your organization views change, whether current strategies are working or failing, all contribute to determine the level of e-business change your organization can swallow. Some great examples are businesses that are built around the Web. In some cases, these businesses do not bear any relationship to any previous measures of costs, revenue and valuation. They do show that a fresh start, without an existing business model to protect, can produce spectacular results.

Smart things to say

The ingredients

There are some important ingredients to consider in the development of your e-business strategy. These elements have direct input on the development of your strategy, and how much assistance is needed for success to occur (Fig. 6.1).

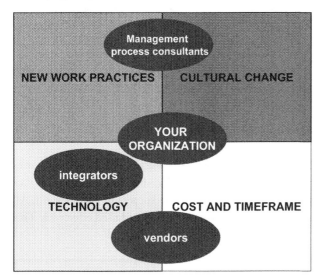

© 2001 The Harvard Computing Group, Inc

Fig. 6.1 Elements and resources impacting e-business and change.

These ingredients make up your plan and strategy. Look at them carefully and see how they might influence your plans (Table 6.3).

Table 6.3 Ingredients for an e-business strategy.

Element and resource	Why they are important
New work practices	Ensure that the program will be supported by documented and agreed new ways of working
Cultural change	Many e-business systems require significant change in the way that an organization does business. Often these are not always complementary with the current culture and practices.
Technology	The technology provides the infrastructure and components for an e-business system. This needs to be developed and deployed to meet the new business, work process and quality goals of the organization.
Cost and timeframe	These are the commitments that you will gain from the development of your strategy and its supporting plan. Without a project plan, you have no way of measuring progress or success ratios for the program. *Do not leave home without one.*
Vendors	Suppliers of technology or Internet e-business services
Integrators	Professional services companies that will provide you with technology advice and development services.
Management work process consultants	Sometimes these services will be available from the Integrator, but often are procured separately. These consultants will provide you with the road map and guide you through the development planning and work process changes critical for success of the system.

Who to influence and why?

Finding the right sponsors and supporters is a crucial element for your e-business strategy. Your starting place is the identification of these individuals. These are the ones who can *guarantee* the success of your system. All systems are successful because they are supported and used effectively This success starts at the beginning, by involving the involved.

SMART THINGS
TO DO

Build a list of those staff in the three groups critical to the project's success and keep them engaged throughout the project.

The statistics of why many systems fail are no different in e-business than with other technologies – except that the results may be more dramatic and horrific in nature, due to the wide-ranging impact of the technology. Every organization needs the following three groups on board for any program to be successful.

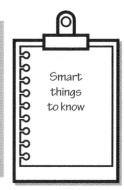

WHO TO INVOLVE IN THE DECISION PROCESS

- Technical staff (the IT department, MIS, CIO or others influencing this process).
- Operational managers of the organization affected by the system, (development, manufacturing, sales, marketing, support, logistics, administrative, HR et al).
- Executive(s). Someone at the executive level to champion the cause in the organization, who is committed and will support the project.

Smart things to know

Almost all failed IT projects have some level of problem with the support of the above groups. Always start by identifying individuals from these groups in your own organization.

Technology awareness

In order to make any intelligent decision about e-business, some technology and work practice education are needed. The first place to start is with a basic understanding of the technology components and how they have helped other companies. By learning from others' experiences, both positive and negative, a framework of understanding is created. This helps us understand where to go and why we should go there. We call this understanding "technology awareness." Technology awareness allows staff to understand not just what the technology can do, but the true *relevance* of the technology to your industry and situation.

SMART THINGS TO DO

When building technology awareness in the organization, ensure that each program *clearly illustrates* the relevance of the technology to your business or organization's needs.

Building technology awareness in your organization provides a foundation for the development of your strategy. It also provides the opportunity to begin team building within the project; without it, gaining consensus in any group can be very difficult.

This approach can be used to ensure that the project is successful from the outset. Understanding some of the fundamentals will be useful to your getting started. Managers and others are much less likely to buy into a program unless they understand what is going on. Traditional means of keeping up to date with what technology is out there for the organization does not play well for a Web-based environment.

Developing a technology-awareness program for the organization can be as simple as attending a seminar, or it could be arranging visits from consulting operations to outline what is involved in the development of an e-business system. Here are a few suggestions to start the ball rolling:

Important elements

The most important element of a program such as this is to demystify the complex areas in the e-business space so that staff can start thinking in an

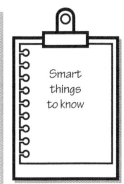

WHY TECHNOLOGY AWARENESS IS IMPORTANT:

- There are too many technology components involved in even a simple e-business solution.
- The packaging of these technologies is changing weekly. A full time analyst would be required for most companies to stay current with the components relevant to them.
- E-business is changing the landscape of many business deals and operations. As the ultimate weapon in an IT arsenal, most firms cannot keep pace with the developments.
- Operational managers and executives in particular have very little time to dedicate to the subject of staying current with technology developments.
- Understanding how competitors and others are using technology to improve their operations is becoming mandatory, not optional.

open and exciting way about how to use the technology. One major method of ensuring that this happens is to keep programs focused on the business aspect of the technology.

- Build a small library of relevant books and articles (see appendices for suggestions).
- Hire an e-business consultant to create a dedicated briefing, specific for your industry.
- Ask one (or more) of your current suppliers to create a briefing for the relevant staff (be careful here, as the supplier will only pitch their products, and provide a less than independent view of the world).
- If you have a training department already in place, ask them to organize a short program on the subject.

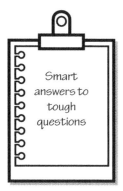

Smart
answers to
tough
questions

Q: How long should technology awareness take?

A: Dependent on the size of your operation, it could take a couple of days, or it may take weeks. As with many of these issues of change in the organization, getting people to the table can take much longer. However, without some form of technology awareness program in place, procurements can take 12 months or more just to start building some consensus for the new program.

Looking for opportunities in the organization

One of the most wonderful aspects of e-business is looking for places to use it. There are so many opportunities waiting for organizations to take advantage of e-business that finding them is usually not the problem. Deciding which you are going to act on is usually a bigger deal.

SMART THINGS
TO DO

As you scour the organization for opportunities to apply e-business, start at the top. Pick the top six things the organization is trying to achieve or change as your starting point. It will *almost ensure* executive support.

Firstly, set your mind at the starting gate. I personally like to start with whatever are the six most important things a company or organization is trying to achieve. Once these are identified, you have already achieved one of the most important elements for success with your program: *the support of your executives*. By picking the leading problems/goals facing the company, and looking for ways e-business is likely to assist in dealing with them, you are already on the right road. By taking this approach, it is also possible to avoid being sidetracked by nice departmental avenues, which may be less important to the leaders in your organizations.

SMART PLACES TO LOOK FOR OPPORTUNITIES

Look for opportunities that support primary business goals, e.g. improve customer support:

- increase sales and client base;
- shorten product development timelines;
- reduce inventory;
- expand partnership network; and
- reduce publishing costs.

Map the opportunities to individual departments and functions:

- try to describe how e-business might help;
- gain agreement with department members; and
- rate the opportunities against business goals.

Review the opportunities with the executive(s):

- begin to quantify the process; and
- illustrate the opportunities and relevance to the business.

Once you have reached this stage, it is possible to then begin the process of mapping them together in an e-business opportunity framework. This will become the building block for the development of the whole strategy.

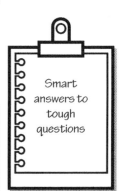

Smart answers to tough questions

Q: Who should I ask for help with my strategy?

A: Start by talking to your customers. Understanding what they want and how they would like it delivered will provide insight, buy-in and input to your e-business system that will be invaluable.

As you can see from Table 6.4, by selecting an area you can then map out how it can be leveraged within your e-business framework.

Table 6.4 Example of e-business opportunity framework.

E-business opportunity	How and where to leverage
Improve customer support	Web-based customer management systems, knowledge bases, on-line information delivery, externalization of current internal customer support information; improved work practices at help desk level.
Increase sales and client base	Web-based marketing, one-to-one marketing, personalization, interactive configuration management via Web, secure transactions for purchases via the Web.
Reduce publishing costs	Provide information in customized form via the Web, generate PDF files for information delivery, use document management technology to distribute appropriate information to parties in electronic form, reduce mail and packaging costs

SMART THINGS
TO DO

Develop an e-business opportunity framework. This includes the opportunity and a basic description of what e-business technology and other changes are needed to support it.

Once you have the e-business opportunity in place, start to review the document with other departmental staff relevant to the function. As you do this, your strategy should start to take shape. It will also start to gain support for the next stages.

Gaining support for your ideas

As the ideas start to become more quantified, it is likely that you will then start to sell them internally. One area to avoid is the actual selling of these ideas as an individual crusade. Any e-business system, even the simplest one, has many variables that can generate results, both positive and negative.

Most e-business systems require many areas of the organization to participate in complex ways; it is very important not to oversimplify just to gain early support in the process.

At this stage is it important to review how each of these components should come together for the total system. As Figure 6.2 illustrates, business goals, technology, new work processes and the final system need to work together in unison. This unification is an important element for all involved to understand in the decision-making process.

Important factors in decision making strategy

Business   Technology   Process   Application

© 2001 The Harvard Computing Group, Inc

Fig. 6.2 Important factors in decision-making strategy.

> Involve groups around the organization early in the process. The later that you do this, the greater the effort will be required to gain buy-in and acceptance for the project.

SMART THINGS
TO DO

Once these ideas are documented and have gained support from your limited sphere of influence, then you can move on selling them internally. Some good examples of ways to make this happen are:

SMART THINGS
TO DO

- Lunch-time briefings (these can be open and informal, and can involve operational managers, execs and others from whom you are soliciting input).
- Departmental and organization-wide meetings to discuss the potential of the technology and where it can be applied.
- Posting on the company intranet (if you have one) in discussion group areas.
- Company newsletters and email to outline strategy and gain feedback.
- Internal Web sites and discussion groups.

Checkpoint

At this stage, you should have achieved the following:

- Identified the appetite for change within the organization and built your strategy around something that will fly.

- Gained a reasonable level of technological awareness within the working group on the relevant technology.

- Documented several potential areas in the organization that can use e-business effectively to support organizational and departmental goals.

- Started to communicate these ideas through the organization.

Building the business case

So now you have some opportunities identified with at least some general support in the organization. An important next step is to quantify the potential outcome, or build a business case to support the initiative.

Building the business case for the e-business strategy is a fundamental step for success. This can be as simple as a few bullet slides and a spreadsheet, but is an essential step to creating effective solutions. E-business applications often provide very high return on investment, many producing returns in the range of 500–2000% or more. These successful ones create tremendous value for the clients.

Many models exist to develop a solid business case, but most require clear measurement of expected outcomes from the implementation. Discussion groups and workshops are often used to ensure consensus and agreement in determining the outcome of e-business systems.

Development of the business case begins with taking the information you have captured so far, and integrating it into a format that can show the business needs, costs and benefits associated with the project.

Table 6.5 Examples of factors to be considered in the development of the e-business business case.

Business needs	Incremental costs	Soft benefits	Hard benefits
Increased sales	Hardware and software costs	Improved competitiveness	Increased sales
New product	Consulting costs (internal/external)	Customer satisfaction	Shorter sales cycles
Greater market penetration	Marketing and promotion	Better access to information	Improved margins
New business initiatives	Hosting and Internet access costs	Improved corporate image	Reduced costs
	Training and implementation	Increased staff satisfaction	

Source: Harvard Computing Group 2001

In general, hard benefits can and should be measured in terms of budgetary impact to the organization. In other words; real money. Other benefits that have a good contributory effect on the operation can be considered soft benefits, not measurable in financial terms. When quantifying savings and potential outcomes I recommend that you are conservative on savings and aggressive on costs.

<table>
<tr><td>SMART THINGS
TO DO</td><td>When estimating costs and benefits, be conservative on savings and aggressive on costs.</td></tr>
</table>

Now that we are getting to where "the rubber meets the road," finding the best way of getting this information down and how it can be quantified is a key element to the success of your project.

Capturing the information

Now we come to the hard part. Getting the information. To develop a business case for any major technology program, but particularly e-business, you must be ready to break down some walls in the organization. First place to start is to involve the right people in the process. Without exception, the process will be slower and more fraught with danger if you do not involve:

- the appropriate executives who could support (or kill) your ideas;

- operations managers who could support (or kill) your ideas; and

- IT staff and management who could support (or kill) your ideas.

<table>
<tr><td>SMART THINGS
TO DO</td><td>Invite everyone you need on the team for an e-business party at your home.</td></tr>
</table>

So many projects go south (not good), because they do not have these groups involved in the process. Pulling these groups together in a common framework is another trick that has to be performed. Here are some ideas for making it happen:

- invite everyone over to your house for cocktails (could be expensive);

- set up a workshop forum sponsored by one of the executives to discuss the potential;

- use any internal change management, IT work process team or CIO/IT support team that has expertise, to help develop the business case; and

- hire an external consulting group that can facilitate the business case development.

However you decide to facilitate the development of the business case, the information that you need from this process includes:

- impact on the organization;

- cost analysis;

- savings;

- outline of technology plan;

- new work practices/processes; and

- agreement that can be "burned into" a budget.

SMART THINGS TO AVOID WHEN DEVELOPING AN E-BUSINESS
STRATEGY

Don't:

- underestimate the amount of change required in the organization for the solution to work;
- forget to look at how your competitors and others in the market have evolved their solutions;
- build a strategy that is not based around core business or organizational goals;
- try and "boil the ocean" by trying to include too many functions in the first go around;
- do little or no research on the impact of change;
- try and sell the solution by underestimating costs;
- focus on the wrong elements of e-business;
- forget to include change management in the program;
- sell the system internally without a supporting business case;
- hope that the new business practices will start when the new system starts; and
- become enamored with the technology alone. It should support a business need.

Impact on the organization

Determining how the organization is going to effectively use e-business technology remains the most important and most difficult part of defining the strategy. The multi-faceted nature of e-commerce presents us with many alternatives. Determining exactly which mixture is right for you requires serious review, as decisions made about e-business (and those unmade) will likely affect your organization for years to come. The variables discussed earlier in this chapter – appetite for change, risk aversion, state of the current operation, competition and financial stability – all change the geography of this landscape. Now will be the time to review the variables and package them together to determine positive (and some negative) outcomes from your strategy.

Table 6.6 illustrates some of the components that make up these changes, and thereby cause much work to be considered for the development of the strategy.

Table 6.6 E-business factors influencing the development of the business case.

e-business factors and components					
People	Influencers	The client (Consumer)	Client (Business-to-business)	Advertisers	Internal staff
Processes	Sales process	Market feedback	Advertising and promotion	Customer support	Maintenance of site
Content	The product	The service	Marketing and catalog information	Legal agreements and contracts	Corporate information
Technology	Infrastructure and development platforms	Security	Content Management	Multi-language support	Hosting and access
Transactions	Purchase	Electronic Funds Transfer (payment)	Fulfillment	Shipping	Taxation

Cost analysis

Once you understand the opportunities and the specific applications identified, your next objective is to measure the savings related to the implementation of the new applications. The starting point is to measure and estimate these at two stages. This is achieved by documenting the expenses associated with tasks in your current environment and then comparing this with estimated expenses after the system is in place.

By now, you are probably getting the picture. The devil is in the detail with these estimates. It is advisable to be much more conservative with the savings estimates, after all you will be responsible for making them happen in the organization. The good news is there are so many opportunities for improvement (in almost any organization) for e-business, that finding these improvements is not nearly as hard as you might think.

Once you have the savings element under control, the time to consider the cost side of the equation has come. Again, these calculations do not need to be Byzantine, but they must be believable and relevant to your operations accounting and procurement rules.

Estimating costs

Having identified the applications and estimated how they will be applied, the next stage is to estimate the costs of buying or building, implementing, and supporting the new e-business applications.

To build a good estimate, start with all of the components. Table 6.7 shows some examples of ones that you should factor into the system.

Identification of the components and estimating the incremental staff resources provide the framework for the estimate. With these we can consider the one-time costs. Wherever possible, use existing systems or platforms to support the needs of the system.

The second step is to estimate the cost of the technology infrastructure that will support all of the applications. Ideally, the goal is to identify a common infrastructure for all applications. An infrastructure that supports many of

Table 6.7 Building a good estimate.

COST ESTIMATE COMPONENTS	
Hardware:	Server, Desktop, Network, Routers, Gateways
Software:	Server, Desktop, Network. One-time purchase or development costs.
Development and Implementation:	One-time consulting, database population, conversion, training, and testing costs.
Support (maintenance):	Annual System administration, hosting services, support, and maintenance costs.

the applications will allow its cost to be distributed and measured against the savings or revenue derived from the applications that it supports. A spreadsheet is also used to capture the system requirements and costs of the base infrastructure. This is considerably more detailed.

Q: How can I reduce additional costs introducing e-business systems into the organization?

A: One way is to re-use existing infrastructure and systems that are already in place. It is likely that some standards are already in place for Web servers, databases, browsers and application development tools. If you can use these tools in your solutions, the adoption and maintenance costs of the system will be greatly reduced.

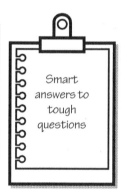

Smart answers to tough questions

Calculating return on investment (ROI)

Calculating the return on investment is, in some ways, the easy part. Once you have identified better methods of working, projected savings and what it will cost, you merely need to put the numbers together. Often the most difficult aspect of calculating the ROI is putting the numbers together in a way that meets your own organization's financial and budget policies. For example, payback periods may vary depending upon how capital purchases are treated and amortized in the organization. In addition, the organization's cash flow may require the cost of borrowing money to be included in the equation.

The technology plan

An outline of the technology plan should also be included in the business plan. This does not have to be detailed at the application specification level but should reflect the components and how they would work with other components of the system.

This can be as simple as a diagrammatic view of the system, as shown below. However, it should illustrate that the basic components have been identified and how they will work in the system.

New work practices and business processes

Determining the new work practices and business processes associated with the system should be an important part of the program. These can be as simple as defining site and product pricing updates, or as complex as defining business-to-business protocols and work processes with distribution and development partners. Part of the successful definition of the business case is to intensively review these procedures when determining the business case. What is the use of spending thousands of dollars on an e-business Web site, and have no method to deliver the goods?

Some of the factors listed above will help identify where to begin considering change in the process. Many of these factors may have little to do with the transaction itself, but can speed the decision-making process, or acceler-

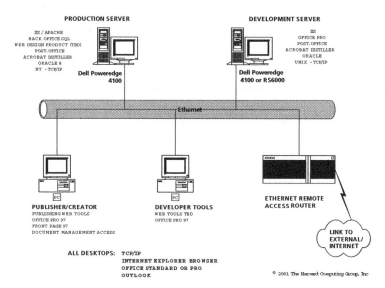

PRODUCTION SERVER

IIS / APACHE
BACK OFFICE SQL
WEB DESIGN PRODUCT (TBD)
POST.OFFICE
ACROBAT DISTILLER
ORACLE 8
NT - TCP/IP

Dell Poweredge 4100

DEVELOPMENT SERVER

IIS
OFFICE PRO
POST.OFFICE
ACROBAT DISTILLER
ORACLE
UNIX - TCP/IP

Dell Poweredge 4100 or RS6000

Ethernet

PUBLISHER/CREATOR
PUBLISHING WEB TOOLS
OFFICE PRO 97
FRONT PAGE 97
DOCUMENT MANAGEMENT ACCESS

DEVELOPER TOOLS
WEB TOOLS TBD
OFFICE PRO 97

ETHERNET REMOTE ACCESS ROUTER

LINK TO EXTERNAL/ INTERNET

ALL DESKTOPS: TCP/IP
INTERNET EXPLORER BROWSER
OFFICE STANDARD OR PRO
OUTLOOK

© 2001 The Harvard Computing Group, Inc

Fig. 6.3 A sample e-commerce system.

ate sales cycles. Business-to-business e-business represents a huge part of the marketplace. E-business provides the opportunity for companies to improve and cement business partnerships, and develop new relationships by offering improved service and support.

Many business processes are linked to what are known as self-service or personalization applications. These are designed to provide information directly to the person who needs it without further intervention. Customer support applications are very popular for these areas, along with a supporting knowledge base to provide the information to the customer when they need it.

Business processes cannot be ignored. If they are, e-business applications may actually increase costs and provide little or no benefit to anyone involved. The strategy will provide the drivers for change, new business processes must be developed to support it.

Gaining agreement and building a phased approach

By now, we can assume that you have gained agreement from the others now comprising your e-business team. You will have probably have identified more opportunities and applications that can make a difference to the organization. Once this happens, one final level of prioritization should be made. This will allow you to take a phased approach to the project, ensuring that the order and scope will be successful.

To build a phased approach:

- prioritize;

- select several tasks and applications that are high value and easy to implement;

- pick some high visibility items that ensure that the team will have success and start working effectively together; and

- break the project into the following time-lines 0–3 months, 3–6 months, greater than 6 months.

Most e-business business decisions are being made in Internet time. Making your move does not necessarily mean high risk and long time frames. Careful choice of strategy and plan can allow to you to move fast and in the right direction.

WHEN DEVELOPING AN E-BUSINESS STRATEGY:

- ensure that you have management support for the project;
- involve the appropriate parties;
- make sure that all involved have a good understanding of the technology, and the way the operation may have to change to support it;
- focus on high-return, high-profile opportunities;
- think out-of-the-box in reviewing alternatives;
- prioritize alternatives based on business or organizational goals;
- develop and agree a budget (by whatever means);
- document the business case; and
- develop a phased approach.

7
Making it Happen – Doing E-Business

We are coming into the closing straight where the rubber meets the road. Recently, I had a meeting with a leading financier of Internet start-up firms. This individual normally takes great care to ensure that he has relevant research information about the investment and the market that the firm is going after. In reviewing the business plan for a potential investment, he asked me whether it was necessary to do any market research for the firm in question. His argument was simple, if they can sign up 10,000 users in three months, with a powerful business argument, and the product is being accepted, who cares about targeting the marketplace. As Nike might say "Just do it!"

Now, this is not to advise that recommendations covered in previous chapters are not relevant, but it does show that we continue to face comparisons with e-business strategies that do not reflect traditional market situations. Knowing whom our client base is and why they will want to do business with us is still critical. At some point however, we have to go for it.

Once we reach this point, we have to make some decisions. The first one is how much help from the outside do I need? A lot, is often the answer for many companies.

Build versus buy

The first decision to be made is the build-versus-buy one. In most cases, we all need some help through the decision cycles. As many businesses are now on their second or third generation of e-business systems, the mistakes of the first time may now appear obvious. As each e-business system requires some significant blend of business, technology and work-process change, it is likely that you will need some outside help. Dependent on the requirements of the project, decisions have to be made where help is needed.

A number of variables determine how much of an individual project should use external resources. These will alter according to the importance of particular functions to the success of the system, and how much control the organization wants to have over these elements. In many financial applications for example, companies want to have total control over the computer systems for a variety of regulatory, security and business process reasons. However, many companies in other industries can take advantage of the wholesale outsourcing of their projects.

Reviewing various aspects of the project provides guidelines for determining which elements are targets for external support or assistance. Table 7.1 illustrates some of these elements and some different resource allocation in a typical e-business project.

These examples reveal where resources could be allocated in this model. As recently as a few years ago, most complex systems involved a tremendous amount of intricate programming in their development. Today there is a

Table 7.1 The potential divisions of labor when making buy-versus-build decisions.

Technology Awareness	Business requirements	Application specification	Project Management	Development	Training	Help Desk	Support	Administration
SIGNIFICANT OUTSOURCING OF THE DEVELOPMENT AND SUPPORT OF THE E-BUSINESS SYSTEM								
INTERNAL	INTERNAL	COMPLETE OUTSOURCING OF ALL TECHNICAL AND SUPPORT FUNCTIONS						
NO OUTSOURCING OF SERVICES, JUST LIMITED ASSISTANCE IN THE DEFINITION AND SECTION OF TECHNOLOGY COMPONENTS								
EXTERNAL			INTERNAL RESOURCES					
MIXTURE OF INTERNAL AND EXTERNAL RESOURCES FOR VARIOUS STAGES OF THE PROJECT								
EXTERNAL	EXTERNAL	EXTERNAL	EXTERNAL	INTERNAL	EXTERNAL	INTERNAL	INTERNAL	INTERNAL

great opportunity to reduce the amount of programming required in the development and even the hosting of the project. Before deciding to "become your own expert" in each one of these areas, review Table 7.2, which illustrates how many of these functions can be outsourced today.

SMART THINGS TO CONSIDER IN A BUY-VERSUS-BUILD DECISION

- Do I have the resources to define the system requirements and the work process needs?
- Has my organization the appropriate development resources and experience to build our e-business systems?
- How much of our existing systems are involved in the development or deployment of an e-business solution?
- How will the content be maintained and updated?
- Who will administer and control the system after it is installed?
- Do we have existing products that could provide the foundation of a new system?

Smart things to think about

The last chapter dealt with many of the issues in the development of the strategy and how to build the business case. Now decisions have to be made that are critical to the success of the systems. Selecting your partners to work with will be an essential component of this system.

Selecting partners

Selecting the right partners to work with is one of the most important decisions in the entire process. Here are some guidelines for what to look for in the development of successful partnerships, in the selection both of the technology vendors and of the consultants that you hire to assist with the implementation.

Table 7.2 Factors for selecting partners for e-business initiatives.

Selection issue	Areas of concern						
Platform support	Operating system	Network operating standard	Compliance with standards	Web support	Thin client	NPR – no programming required	Use and compatibility with leading programming systems
Financial viability	Is e-business a core business?	Well funded	Profitable				
Quality	References	Reliability of systems	Release schedules	Time for critical fixes	Escalation procedures	Test drive the help desk	Knowledge Base
Price	Licensing scheme	Cost per seat	Maintenance cost	Server base pricing	Web pricing	Partner program	
Performance	Number of transactions	Impact on desktop	Network performance	Remote access	Database engine	Overhead	Scalability
Business practices	Integrity	Pricing policies	Guarantees	References	Attentiveness	Quality of staff	Responsiveness
Support	Help desk	Standard support contracts	Response times	Consulting support	Training	Local offices	
Maintenance	Cost of administration	Software distribution	Fixes policy and guarantee period	Cost of maintenance, Help desk, Fixes, Updates	Frequency of updates		
Cost of ownership	Set up costs	Training investment, Initial, Ongoing	Internal help desk Initial Ongoing	Annual maintenance costs	Dependencies		

These factors will have a major impact on the success of your system deployment.

Platform support

Ensuring that all decision-making staff are familiar with your organization's platform plans is very important. This can influence results in time and performance. If your organization already has standards in place, it makes sense to use these as the baseline for new systems technology. For example, if a particular Web server or database is available and supported in the organization, then pick companies that have products and staff familiar with these standards. Many organizations will tout their services as being "open," however this often means that they will use whatever you want, but may be learning these products for the first time on your "dollar." This not only increases costs, but will also compromise timeframes and the quality of the results. It usually makes sense to do business with an organization that already has skills in a particular area, even if they are not as "open" as some other firms.

Financial viability

Avoid doing business with companies that are not financially sound. However, in the Internet space, many products are developed and brought to market by innovative start-ups that can cut months off a systems development timeline and reduce maintenance costs. (Many content-management systems are in this category, with few vendors in the market for more than 24 months). Careful consideration should be made to understand the financial backing of companies in this space, although most that are now in the market have been there for some time.

Quality

Quality of product and services remains an important decision point for doing business with a company. As a significant amount of your firm's business is likely to be tied to the success of this system, paying attention to quality is paramount. In particular among product companies, examine references (in similar applications if possible), and release schedules (notoriously subject to slippage), and talk to user groups or communities if possible. Many companies now have a great deal of customer support materials and services available on-line. Look at their bulletin boards, FAQ databases, knowledge bases and other support programs provided to help their clients after systems have been installed and supported.

Pricing

Everyone is sensitive to price when developing a new system. Pricing dynamics and the Internet are continually changing phenomena. In general, software is still sold using server-based pricing, with a license charge according to the number of users of the system. (There are some variations to this model, but in the main, this continues to be a common practice). Some firms now will offer combined services, where the software, maintenance and the hosting of the system are included in the price. (This will vary according to the amount of traffic, users or transactions of the system.)

Price comparisons have to take into account various factors that affect each other in e-business pricing. These can be exceptionally complex; nevertheless, it is an important exercise. With many Internet offerings, firms want to engage you with their platform at the entry price, but then expand their offerings (read revenue), as your system needs grow. This is not necessarily a bad thing, but it makes it even more important to compare apples with apples at this early stage of the procurement.

Smart things to think about

PRICING COMPARISONS

Incremental software costs:

- product costs;
- annual maintenance costs; and
- staffing costs for internal support.

Development and deployment costs:

- timeframe;
- type of contract (fixed price, time and materials);
- maintenance costs; and
- hosting.

Performance and scalability

Even the best-designed systems fail. Performance of your e-business solution for clients and potential partners will be the criterion for early success or failure of the project. It is amazing how little patience consumers have today for systems that have long load times, poor performance or other factors that make the experience bad. Of course, if the system is not up and running when the consumer or client wants to use it, then no amount of "under construction" signs will help you out. From what we know today about the habits of Internet consumers, we know that the companies who have been successful understand the importance of making the experience a fulfilling and pleasant one. Performance is crucial to getting this right.

Part of this process is picking a system and architecture that is scalable, and can be expanded quickly and easily. Fortunately, most systems are now built on n-tier architectures that will provide scalability and dramatic improvements in performance, with little changes to the architecture. Companies in the financial services and the on-line auction business are good examples of systems that have been implemented with this scalability factor in mind. (When one of these systems fails for whatever reason, it becomes national news.)

Business practices

As the partners that you pick for e-business are likely to be around for a while, making sure that you get on well with each other is a critical factor in the relationship. Unlike many other technologies, we can expect to see a lot of change occurring in the systems that are developed. For this reason, it is even more important that flexibility, trust and partnership are all part of the relationship. When changes are required to e-business systems, they are usually required quickly. Therefore, building relationships with partners that can provide speedy responses to rapidly changing market conditions is very important.

Also, as many systems require deep and confidential knowledge of your business operations and strategy, having partners that you can truly trust, in more than just the legal sense, is imperative.

Support

The proper support in place for any e-business solution is often the difference between success and failure. The various flavors of support that will be needed include:

- help desk;

- training and technology transfer;

- on-site support; and

- client support.

Depending on the amount of support that you plan to have outside the company, there may be different business models to meet support needs. Some firms will outsource all but the essential aspects of the system, others will want everything in their control and for it to be internal. Vendor and integrator cycle times and escalation procedures need to be reviewed carefully to see if they meet the needs of your operation. As it is likely that you will have several vendors, and perhaps one or two consulting operations assisting with the system, keeping the support criteria built to standards that meet the business needs has consequences. (For example if one vendor commits to a four-hour response on critical problems, and another's response is 24, the 24-hour response becomes the new low point for critical support.)

Maintenance

Maintaining an e-business system has many facets. Some of the more obvious ones have already been reviewed earlier. Here are the dimensions to the issue:

- software updates and administration of systems;

- updates and delivery to the clients and users of the system; and

- maintaining content, policy and pricing.

While the first two are in the category of issues that all system administrators have to deal with, the latter provides a great opportunity for flexibility and cost reduction.

If a vendor or integrator requires their own staff to make changes to the system and its content as the *only* way of updating the system, *beware*. Many organizations have locked themselves into systems that are difficult to change, update and modify. These relationships cause problems, are based on old models of content maintenance and should be avoided at all costs. One major problem, with this type of system, is that the funnel for the information delivery and publishing process is still the old one, often based on paper-based publishing and information release. In general, most systems should drive the content maintenance back to the desktop of the individual responsible for the material and they should have the ability to change this "anywhere in the world." Dynamic and effective content maintenance and development is critical for success.

Cost of ownership

Developing a cost model that reflects these various decision points, and using the examples in Chapter 6, a predictive summary of costs can be delivered to the potential decision makers.

As part of this exercise, illustrating why these will have an ongoing effect on cost of ownership has several benefits:

- it will help you differentiate offerings from different vendors and suppliers; and

- ongoing training and support costs can be compared with different strategies. For example comparing outsourcing versus internal support of the system.

Integration with the existing Internet infrastructure

A great place to start determining the road ahead is to review exactly what you have in place right now. This may seem like a complex task, particularly if you are not a "techie" familiar with all the vagaries of this world. However, even a simple checklist of items to look for when determining the technical strategy can help.

MAKE A CHECKLIST FOR BUILDING E-BUSINESS SOLUTIONS

- Web servers in use;
- Web development and authoring tools used for existing Internet solutions;
- back office systems;
- database products and standards;
- communication tools and protocols; and
- e-mail and messaging standards.

SMART THINGS
TO DO

This short list can provide an excellent starting point for the development of new systems. Most IT organizations will have some preferences and standards in place, even in the smallest organizations. By understanding what is in place initially, costs can be reduced and support can be generated from the IT group by bringing them into the picture early. Of course, there may well be many components that will be considered here that are not part of any existing systems. Software components such as e-business application servers, transaction servers and more sophisticated Web analysis tools would be included in this category.

E-Commerce Infrastructure

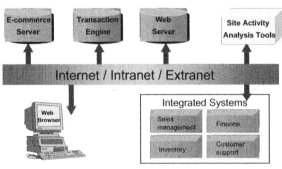

©1999 The Harvard Computing Group, Inc.

Fig. 7.1 Components of the e-business system.

Understanding these integration requirements early in the process also allows for a more co-orientated project-management process. A great deal of success is usually dependent on the support and assistance from the internal IT department.

Content management and its role in electronic business

Content management and content are words regularly misunderstood. In the early stages of Web development, most content was funneled and delivered to the Webmaster. The Webmaster became the center of the world for the development, administration, support and content management of the site. This model failed miserably. It has caused enormous frustration inside organizations about their ability to make changes occur in a timely manner for site information. The other side caused burnout to occur with Web masters who were suddenly faced with policy decisions, editors, spell checkers and chief arbitrators of what was or was not done.

The reason for this problem is that the Web was initially viewed as a giant publishing system, but instead of overcoming the problem with the technology, new work processes were put in place to get it to happen fast. However, there was no logic to this, hence the problem.

Some of these problems were also exacerbated by the early stage of Web development tools. Essentially the market focused on individual authoring tools (such as FrontPage, PageMill, HotDog and others).

The early versions of these tools put the power of HTML authoring in the hands of individuals, but did not work well in the workgroup scenario. In addition, people that owned the content and needed to change and update it did not have the tools they needed. Hence the bottleneck.

Today, thankfully there are many tools to address this issue. While there is still a need for Web masters to have control over how content is published and managed, (at least from the technical viewpoint), there is little need for them to be involved in the change management process associated with content and how it will be presented. Ideally, this should be driven back to the authors and reviewers associated with this process.

Smart things to know

Automated content-management tools are the answer to this problem. Thankfully they are now becoming abundantly available in the marketplace and can be tightly integrated into an e-business system from the beginning.

Many organizations have encounted significant problems maintaining their Web-based systems. Content management is rapidly becoming a major issue for many firms to deal with the appropriate maintenance and effectiveness of their Web sites. Content management is about the control of data. Data is content, and content is material that needs to be customized, presented and collected by users of the system.

Content-management systems are built specifically to improve the way those companies interact with, and control their Web-based applications. They are usually selected when three factors are present in the organization's Internet strategy. These are:

- interactive content;

- distributed information; and

- customized content.

When to use them

Content-management system purchases are often driven by the need for electronic business or e-business. The types of application being developed include catalogs and product information sites, business-to-business applications, self-service and customer-service applications. These usually require careful control and presentation of information providing the most value to the target consumer and, at the same time, require close control of the update, release, and approval processes for the information on the site.

Customers using content management systems want control and speed. They want quality and customization of both content and appearance. Fortunately, with the modular nature of many content-management systems, it is possible to have it all. Content-management systems provide the business controls to manage the data presentation, enable distributed updating, and make posting new changes fast yet customized.

Content-management systems provide a framework to control information. They link the authoring, approval, editing and the release (Web publishing) processes. Typically, the sorts of problems that are solved by content-management systems include:

- control of updates (in the hands of the content approver, not just the Web master);

- interactive content which keeps the Web site fresh and relevant; and

- support of the business needs of the operation by providing *control* over the customization of content for many applications and users.

Options

One choice that many organizations are faced with today is to decide whether to go with a document, publishing or business-oriented system. While for some applications the choice may not make a difference, others will clearly benefit from a particular selection. Table 7.3 illustrates some examples to help you decide:

Table 7.3 Content management system options.

Customer application	Application characteristics	Best suited system
Technical publishing, database publishing, knowledge management applications	High volume electronic document applications. Built-in sophisticated information retrieval and PDF generation	Document oriented Content Management
Catalogs, business-to-business applications, supply-chain and distribution applications	Customization of content and presentation can be controlled interactively. Business rules can be developed and modified easily. High level of personalization.	Business oriented Content Management
Commercial publishing, electronic magazines and personalized content.	Customized content can be presented in many different forms and formats.	Publishing oriented Content Management

Legacy systems

As organizations look at e-business strategies, they often consider starting with a blank sheet of paper. This of course is not often the case, (unless the company is a new start-up, and even start-ups have some existing materials).

Although the term has become a little abused in recent years, a legacy system is generally described as an existing computer system that is providing a function for some part of the business. Sometimes, these systems are considered as older in nature, but often provide some strategic function to the business. Examples might include:

- inventory management systems;

- manufacturing resource planning systems (MRP);

- enterprise resource planning (ERP);

- sales automation systems; and

- help desk systems.

It is interesting that many firms now consider their client/server applications legacy systems. Legacy systems often provide a great resource of information to assist with the building of e-business systems. Some examples include:

Table 7.4 Examples of legacy systems and how they can be used in e-business solutions.

Legacy system	Application
Sales automation	Client information base for new e-business activities
Inventory management system	Ability to externalize this information to partners and end user clients as part of an extranet solution
Customer Help Desk system	Could be used as a browser based interface to an Internet customer management system
MRP	Access to the MRP system can allow clients to place order on-line and get information on delivery timelines for special orders

LEGACY SYSTEMS

- Look for databases that can provide continuity with your e-business requirements.
- Review departmental databases (marketing, sales, customer support) that have potentially useful seed information for your project.
- Investigate major transaction- and business-critical databases and systems as part of your plan. Excluding them could cause significant reductions in productivity in future stages of the e-business plan.
- Look for the support of standards such as XML to support interoperability between systems.

Smart things to know

International considerations

By now, most companies have implemented a presence on the Web. For many, an important aspect of this decision was the capability to go worldwide with their message and product. However, the global nature of the Web prohibits many firms from making the "big move" to international e-business. Many decisions have to be taken before putting US price lists out there for the world to see. To achieve accelerated sales cycles, potential clients have to see more information in order to make decisions quickly. Meanwhile, corporate concerns about comparative shopping and the public broadcast of previously "private" information, all gnaw at the current culture of the organization.

These issues, and more, come to the fore when considering international e-business solutions. Determining the timing and methods to implement a program that will be successful can be a daunting task. The Web can be a short cut, but there is a huge difference in an "informational site," and using the Web as an integrated part of a company's international business.

The road to success may be paved in part, but there are also some road repairs that can make the journey hazardous.

The fundamentals

Several factors influence the development of an international strategy. These factors are often considered separately, but for a successful implementation should be considered in a common framework.

One reason why companies have taken time to make this move is the widespread impact to the organization, clients and distribution systems. Reviewing international e-business as either technology or as a better way

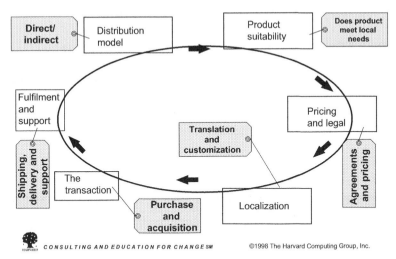

Fig. 7.2 Components of an international e-business strategy.

of doing business can lead to failure. Successful implementations consider both the business and technology factors as one.

Determining the business model

An international e-business strategy can change how a company is doing business in a dramatic way. The requirements for such a change need careful consideration. Ensuring that this effect is dramatic in improvement and not traumatic to others is essential for success.

Usually one of three scenarios form the basis of the business model:

• a new international business on the Web;

- changing an existing international direct sales business model; and

- changing an existing international indirect sales business model.

As Table 7.5 indicates, some major changes have to be considered in the development of this strategy. For companies that already have international distribution in place, channel conflict can be a major concern. For new distribution strategies the other concern of product support also will play a major part in the development of the strategy.

Table 7.5 Business model impact with international e-business.

Business model	Impact on direct sales to new International clients	Impact on current International channels	Impact on direct sales to current International clients
New International e-business business model	No channel conflict, but complete system from demand through fulfillment has to be developed	Not applicable	Not applicable
Existing direct business model (non Web based)	Could create conflict with current distribution systems in place, if not factored into the design.	Not applicable	Could create conflict with current distribution systems in place, if not factored into the design.
Existing indirect business model	Could create conflict with current distribution systems in place, if not factored into the design.	Needs to be developed considering existing channels and support that is in place.	Could create conflict with current distribution systems in place, if not factored into the design.

Source: Harvard Computing Group 2001

Product suitability

Ensuring that a product is suitable for the target marketplace, is the next step in the process. This includes a number of factors that are specific for e-business, but also others that are important to ensure success.

A moderate amount of research should provide the information that will determine the most attractive markets to target. This will also provide some good input on the scale and cost of what is needed to customize your product or service to enter the market.

Table 7.6 Factors affecting product suitability in international marketplace.

	Is product competitive in local marketplace?
Pricing	
Competitiveness	How should product be priced and packaged for local market needs?
Language	Is localization required to enter the market? What will the cost and scope of translation needed for success?
Market size	Is the marketplace large enough to warrant the investment?
Internet infrastructure	Are there a suitable number of Internet users to make the transactions happen? (including good connections via ISPs)
Cultural infrastructure	Is e-business accepted as a means of doing business? What is the current rate of e-business growth in this market?
Existing distribution systems	Are there current distribution systems in place that will help (or hinder) an e-business initiative?
Shipping/fulfillment	How will the product be shipped and delivered to the client?
Support	What local support is required?
Volatility	Is the market volatile? (Either financially or politically)

Source: Harvard Computing Group 2001

Pricing and legal factors

Developing pricing strategies for international distribution via the Web is no more complex (or simple) than any other environment. However, if this is the first foray into the international marketplace, then several issues need to be determined.

The first phase will consist of the basic business issues of:

• single or custom pricing strategy for each market;

- margin goals;

- cost of sale;

- cost of support; and

- market share goals.

Once these have been determined, other pricing factors come into play including:

- competition;

- what will the current marketplace stand?

- currency transactions;

- import duties;

- export duties; and

- shipping costs.

Many companies are concerned that once their US list price is shown on their site, then it will be very difficult to obtain a different (read higher) price from other markets. There is no question that once a US list price is shown, then a benchmark has been placed for international prospects to consider. However, there are other issues to consider that cause changes in price and support.

Some examples of these are shown in Table 7.7.

Table 7.7 Examples of variables and the impact on pricing strategies.

Variables	Impact on pricing
Warranty	Increased price for International support
One single price based on US list	If the transaction is in dollars, no currency issues arise
Support	Local support has different price
Shipping and handling	Cost will increase based on client requirements (air or sea freight)
Customs and import/export duties	Usually paid by the consumer

Source: Harvard Computing Group 2001

Careful consideration of contract issues should to be made to avoid potential problems. A good approach is to keep things simple and understandable. This will reduce confusion and potential problems. Many countries have very different commercial trading practices, and it is important to become familiar with them before presenting them with an unsatisfactory method of purchase.

The legal profession and governments worldwide are trying their best to come to terms with the complex array of problems associated with trading on the Web. The Web changes many rules of trading that were based on the physical transfer of goods across borders for many years.

Cultural change

In earlier chapters we have discussed much about the issue of change, and how it affects our focus on the future. One area never to be underestimated is that of the organizational culture. Determining how best to take advantage of change in the operation is a soft skill. Despite being a soft skill, we often feel like using something harder when trying to convince others to change their behavior.

Developing new systems for e-business requires considerable change in many aspects of a business. The resistance or willingness to deal with these changes can have a major impact on how you go about encouraging others to move down the same path.

Some operations have very conservative approaches built into their cultures, in some cases they have not really had to consider even the basic concerns of competition. In this example, regulated industries such as utilities around the globe, costs and government controls have influenced the behavior of these organizations.

E-business can cause all these things to change; making sure that the organization is ready to make some of these moves needs a preparedness exercise of sometimes larger proportion.

Smart things to think about

ORGANIZATION CULTURE

- How ready is the organization to consider change?
- Will change be readily accepted in the operation?
- What will be the easiest way to gain agreement for major change in the operation?

By understanding the culture in the organization, it is easier to determine where are the points of success are in the operation.

Roadmap and timeline

The roadmap for the development of the system shows the various stages along the way of the selection and deployment program. Timelines obviously vary according to the specific tasks in hand. The development of the business model is a critical aspect to the timing.

Determining the roadmap and timeline for your e-business system requires that business goals, processes and technology be aligned. Many organizations now use workshops, seminars and other consensus-building forums to reach important decisions in a short period. This allows for a rapid development of specification, selection, deployment and rollout of new technologies to the organization. This process dramatically reduces the risk of requirements changing during development, and keeps all participants focused on common goals and objectives.

Most e-business projects may be divided into seven phases:

1   technology awareness;

2   needs-assessment/business-case preparation;

3   functional requirements specification;

4   go-to-market strategy;

5   development;

6   implementation/training; and

7   market roll-out.

Table 7.8 Seven-step checklist with sample timeline.

Technology awareness	Needs assessment/ business case preparation	Functional requirements specification	Go-to-market strategy	Development	Implementation and training	Market roll-out
Week 1	Weeks 2–4	Weeks 4–8	Weeks 8–12	Weeks 12–20	Weeks 20–22	Weeks 22–24

The timeline shown in Table 7.8 is for sample purposes only. However, unlike some more traditional information technology solutions, most e-business applications have to be developed quickly and have to be able to respond to market needs. This factor is very material to most operations with their e-business strategies, as many want to move rapidly, if only because they have already spent too much time considering alternatives with traditional means.

SMART THINGS
TO DO

Avoid:

- lengthy procurement processes that extend the timelines for system decision-making processes;
- releasing generic RFPs that will cause you to "churn" in the evaluation cycle; and
- starting development before you know what you want to build.

Technology awareness

As discussed in Chapter 6, a technology awareness seminar can bring staff from a wide range of backgrounds and interests and get everyone onto the same playing field. In ideal circumstances the seminar will not only cover the relevant technologies for e-business, but also be pertinent to the industry or task in hand.

Needs assessment/business case preparation

In addition to the needs assessment and business-case preparation recommended in Chapter 6, some preliminary review of a go-to-market strategy is also required at this stage. The business case will have to review some aspects of the cost and impact on competitive forces, as the numbers to support the business model become apparent.

The business case includes a summary of the recommendations, high-level descriptions of the applications including the cost, savings, return on investment, payback period, speed to implement, outcomes and hard/soft benefits.

> Q: How can I take months from my decision making and implementation of my e-business system?
>
> A: Define a tight game plan, a short time line that does not add extra steps to the process. Ensure that your e-business needs are well defined early in the process, and tested in the market.

Smart
answers to
tough
questions

Functional requirements and system specification

Once the business case is complete, the company is armed with the information needed to decide which projects should be tackled, create an implementation plan, and complete the *functional requirements specification phase* of the project. During this phase, functional specifications are prepared for all or some of the applications defined in the business case. The specifications may then be distributed to vendors and integrators to receive proposals for hardware, software, development, and/or implementation costs. IT employees may also use the specifications and develop the applications internally.

Many organizations now use workshops to assist with the rapid definition of functional specification. Depending upon the size and scope of the application, workshops may last from a few hours to several days.

The functional requirements specifications include more detailed infrastructure recommendations that are formulated to ensure support of the existing applications and any new or enhanced applications identified in the plan.

KILLER
QUESTIONS

FOR USERS IN BUILDING APPLICATIONS

The recommendations will be defined by evaluating:

- Who uses the application?
- How is the information accessed (internal/remote (home or other offices)?
- What are their interactivity requirements? How often must the information be updated?
- What are the security requirements for the data? What security is available in the user interface, at the server? What are the security requirements for data transmitted using the Internet or intranet? Are there different requirements for email?
- What information must be captured?
- What are the interface requirements, import and export?
- What hardware is currently in use, what are the upgrade plans?
- What are the bandwidth requirements?
- Can, will, or should databases be replicated to decrease bandwidth requirements?
- Is public access a requirement?
- What are the back-up requirements for the information? Are there applications that require redundancy to ensure there are no down times?
- What are the acceptable down times for each application, if any?

Building prototypes

Development of prototypes can help dramatically with gaining agreement on issues of user interfaces, look and feel, addressing the target audience and gaining consensus for the program. Prototypes can consist of sample views of how the site will be navigated and what content will be included.

Using prototypes can:

- ensure that the working group agrees on direction;
- provide a visual aid to show how and where things will be;
- provide great feedback for the Web master in the development process; and
- allow change to occur quickly when necessary.

SMART THINGS
TO DO

While some purists will suggest that prototypes should be developed with the tools with which you plan to develop the system, that is really not necessary. One great value of the myriad authoring tools on the market is that relatively inexperienced individuals can produce sites that have the "look and feel" of a professional one. These tools allow users to change the way that they look by predefined templates, artwork and typographic treatment. Many will have thematic approaches for different industries and audiences.

Go-to-market strategy (GTM)

Arguably, the go-to-market strategy should be considered earlier in the process, as part of the development of the business case, or business plan if the system is part of a new initiative. In most cases, the go-to market-strategy

Fig. 7.3 Example of prototype for new business-to-business e-business site.

is at least refined at this stage, to ensure that all the necessary issues are identified as part of the process. A go-to-market strategy will provide the vehicle to permit the process changes, marketing, sales programs and other promotional aspects of the introduction of the new system to be effective. Often these are left to the last stage after the system has been introduced. When the GTM strategy is integrated into the rest of the program, time is lost and the risks of not meeting expectations are increased dramatically.

Make sure your go-to-market-strategy includes:

- marketing plan and tactical actions;
- press plan and tour;
- introduction to existing and new clients;
- pricing and packaging information;
- site traffic promotion;
- introductory offers (if appropriate);
- partner programs (if appropriate);
- internal promotion and explanation of the new site and purpose; and
- validation of the business model.

One of the major items to continue to test in any e-business solution or offering is the validity of your business offering. Unfortunately, if we had to worry only about the technology changing in the Internet space, life would be relatively easy. The reality is that the business offerings of the Internet are also changing rapidly. Since the spring of 1999, when this book was begun, these two examples show how much is changing and how fast it is changing.

1   *Intranet offerings.* Were offered as licensed products in the spring, now are being offered as hosted products with a zero entry cost.

2   *Extranet collaboration products.* Were offered (and are still offered as licensed software products), but are now also available free with no entry cost as a hosted product.

Most firms are now employing almost real-time target marketing techniques to ensure that their GTM strategy will still be relevant by the time that the product is available. They are also using a variety of specialists in these various areas of e-business development, to create a "virtual team" with experience, in a very short period of time. This type of collaboration is likely to continue, to reduce the time and increase the accuracy of the decision-making processes.

Development

Once the specifications are firm, and the green light is given, development can commence. As mentioned earlier, the issue of maintainability and cost of updating the site can have a profound impact on the quality and approach taken. Many companies have spent significant dollars on the development of their first e-business system, only to find that it does not meet the market needs, and they then have to do the same thing over again. The cost of learning in this business should not be underestimated. However, hiring the best and most appropriate development resources (if you are not doing it in-house) will be money well spent.

Different companies and individuals have various approaches for the best way of building the system. All but the most complex systems are built today in relatively short timeframes. Whatever the timeframes, there is a need to review the work product along the way, and ensure that adequate time has been allocated for testing and quality assurance.

Implementation and training

Once the development is over, the implementation, training and roll-out of the system has to be handled. Many organizations will add a beta-test phase to the program to ensure that good user acceptance of the system will occur. This also allows for further feedback to the characteristics of the e-business system that can "fine-tune" the final application before it is released.

If the usability and navigation aspects of the system have been well designed, there is often no need for user-based training of the product or application. However, there are many business-to-business systems that are considerably more complex than those of the business-to-consumer application on the market; these need product and user training.

SMART THINGS TO DO

Make sure you test the following:

- purchase procedures;
- access controls;
- navigation and critical links;
- affinity and related sites;
- all security aspects of the system;
- pricing;
- configuration management (if applicable);
- legal agreements and contracts; and
- confidentiality and privacy concerns.

Market roll-out

Once the application has been tested effectively, you are now ready to release the system to the world. Launching a site can be an exciting and a trying time for all concerned. Making sure that you are ready is important.

Now is the time when all the work is ready to be really tested. Do not assume that e-business systems are "done" when you reach this phase; this is just the beginning. Change in the e-business world is the norm, being ready and able to change according to market and company needs ultimately defines long-term success.

8
Using Technology in the Enterprise – How Executives Can Change Their Organizations

Given the challenges of today's marketplace, executives are looking for solutions that will give them a key advantage over their competitors. Part of this advantage is clearly based on identifying ways to use technology and innovative work practices to improve the productivity, reduce costs and improve service to employees, partners and consumers. A key element of any strategy today will include creating and managing information using portals as the framework.

CRITICAL FACTORS FOR IT EFFECTIVENESS

These include the following:

- development and support of corporate strategies;
- return on investment;
- competitive edge;
- leverage of core competency ; and
- ability to adapt to changing business conditions.

Technology and business systems – united?

Market conditions change faster than ever before, yet our ability to adapt and deal with them seems to be worse than ever. Despite the fact that information technology solutions are mature and available, the gap between the organization that wins the first time out and the others continues to widen. How can operations such as Cisco and Altra create tremendous value using technology to support their business needs, and yet others spend millions and still fail to get it right? How can one firm be so immensely successful, while others fail?

One way to ensure that benefits are derived from IT systems is to focus on the most strategic applications and tie them into the way that the business is working and needs to work in the future.

The development of new products and the promise of an Internet-based economy have all added to the confusion in the marketplace. Now more than ever, executives need to create game plans that will bring them successfully through potentially challenging market conditions.

We all understand the value of strategy to an organization, but the real value is not just understanding what strategy is, but knowing how to turn a strategy into results. Leading management thinkers such as Peter Drucker, now believe that strategy is one of the most important weapons in the arsenal of any business executive. Given the desire of shareholders and staff alike to create value rapidly, one of the most important skills is to turn this into results. Turning strategy into results requires expertise and techniques that leverage enterprise and individual business function skills into improvement across the board.

Our imaginations could be one of the most important condiments for the next generation of e-business systems. In many cases, the very framework of our existing environments limits us, and thus causes us to consider only solutions that will "fit in." Building successful e-business systems is not an art or a science. It is a blend of people, processes and technology.

Return on investment

A powerful business case and sound ROI is key to ensuring the support of management and the board of directors for large enterprise programs. While it may appear obvious that the development of an ROI business case is an essential element of any successful program, it is amazing how many projects reach the procurement phase without one, and become stalled at this stage. Actually, becoming stalled at this stage may be a good thing, because at least this way they do not become one of the failed statistics discussed earlier. A surprisingly large number of IT projects make it past procurement and reach the development or deployment phase without an ROI, which is exactly why the numbers cited are so high.

In order to gain support for these systems, a clear determination of the ROI model has to be extracted from the process. The following framework should assist others in the development of such a program, based on a consulting methodology used for several years by the Harvard Computing Group, Inc.

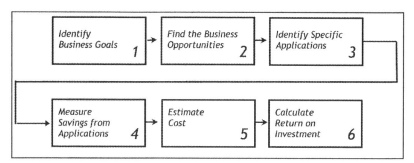

Fig. 8.1 How to develop an effective ROI strategy. Courtesy of Harvard Computing Group, Inc.

This simple, six-stage process creates an effective framework to gain consensus inside the organization to ensure that success will result. As part of this process, it is important to ensure that applications and requirements that do not support the organizational goals die rapidly. All areas of the organization must be focused on meeting the selected requirements; "pet projects" and "special needs" that have self-serving purposes should not be allowed to continue. One of the major problems for many firms is that few organizations have a framework that can assist in the facilitation of these goals. Thankfully, many organizations are taking this process more seriously, and are either installing such programs to develop their systems based on business needs, or are using specialists that understand both the management and technology components of these systems. Either way, organizations have experienced enough failure to know when it has to stop.

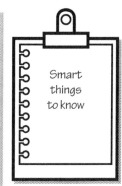

Smart
things
to know

Portal technologies – the cornerstone of most systems

Portals are a very misunderstood topic, and one that many managers and executives have struggled to understand in the context of their organizations. As portals have evolved from the Internet search engines to the corporate desktop, organizations, consultants and vendors have all struggled to define how best to comprehend this important concept and technology. At a corporate level, portals are a "gateway" to a set of information and resources that are part of a specific business environment. The environment could exist for a company's employees, their business partners or consumer groups.

In practical terms, creating a portal involves organizing information around those who need it, so it is available at the time that they need it. For more than ten years the credo of workflow, document or content management software providers has been to deliver the right information, to the right person, at the right time. Portal technologies do not replace the core capabilities of these products. Instead, they help to take this objective even one step further by linking disparate information sources together, regardless of their type, in a meaningful manner, and then delivering them to users' desktops. For many organizations, the concept of managing information based on the role of the individual in the organization is still a new one, but it is one that is growing in strength. Portal technologies are now being deployed in large numbers, as the network of employees, consumers and partners becomes connected via the Internet. Building these systems around the way that organizations work, and making the connections occur quickly is also creating the huge returns for operations that are using them effectively.

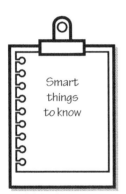

Smart things to know

WHERE TO USE ENTERPRISE TECHNOLOGIES

- Connecting employees with data sources and information relevant to their needs.
- Controlling and expanding knowledge networks.
- Creating business partner networks.
- Reducing operating costs.
- Improving quality and consistency.

Portal technologies that connect people to information, based on their role in the organization, can dramatically improve an organization's ability to make the same content available to others with the same role. Similarly, when business requirements change, role-based portals allow an enterprise to add or change access rights for entire groups of people with minimal effort. In the absence of role-based administration, organizations spend untold hours configuring permissions and access rights for individual applications, databases and content sources.

Recent studies of portal technologies that have been deployed effectively are producing "wake-up calls" around many boardrooms. The ability to connect workers with relevant information in a timely fashion has always been a desirable goal but has been difficult to achieve. During a study con-

Smart
things
to know

ducted by Harvard Computing Group of portal customers, several firms indicated that the improvements in employee effectiveness that resulted from the deployment of the portal were saving up to 15–30 minutes a day per employee. Even for relatively small organizations, the benefits build up very rapidly.

Partner networks are another very effective method of leveraging portal technologies. By linking the information and security requirements for a particular partner in a portal, a company can establish specialized, secure networks in a very short time, allowing firms to be agile and flexible in meeting their partners' requirements. By taking advantage of the security features of portal products, the issues of increased control and dissemination are not mutually exclusive. Organizations can have the benefit of providing selected internal information to their partners, while ensuring that they do not provide more information access than is required.

Competitive edge

In addition to using portal technology inside the organization to improve business operations, firms are deploying portals to gain the upper hand on their competitors. Because organizations can use portals to deliver data, applications and transaction-management systems in a single environment, they are able to deploy complex systems in a relatively short period, thereby getting a jump on their competition.

A recent survey by Morgan Stanley Dean Witter demonstrates that there is enormous opportunity for firms that can succeed in turning their back-office systems to face the customer. The survey indicated that fewer than 41% of CIOs surveyed interact on-line with their clients, and that the majority of firms conduct e-business with only 10% of their suppliers. This leaves a lot of room for those firms that are developing and focusing on the integration of core technologies and then using them as a competitive advantage for their clients.

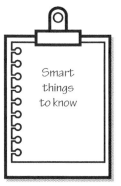

Smart things to know

A recent survey indicated that fewer than 41% of CIOs interact with their clients on-line, and only 10% conduct e-business with their suppliers.

Many significant business improvements are not possible without integrating these back-office systems into a common framework. Portal technologies are fast becoming the vehicle to achieve this goal, leveraging the existing environments and allowing operations to rapidly create customer support systems that dramatically deliver appropriate solutions to the users who need them.

One strategy that really helps organizations build their competitive edge is self-service. Self-service systems allow users to gain access to many different information sources and applications to "serve themselves." Whether it is internal self-service applications, or external to customers or partners, self-service creates value for all concerned. Used effectively, self-service systems allow an organization to develop relationships and facilitate transactions that previously took hours or days.

An example of this self-service program is Krispy Kreme, a large, US-based food retailer who use Corechange's product to distribute relevant sales reports directly to franchisees and divisional directors. Considerable savings were made as a result of this application, and better service to their business partners.

To fully understand the importance of self-service, we have to re-establish some principles that have not been in vogue recently. Due to the meltdown in many dotcom enterprises in late 2000 and early 2001, many bricks-and-mortar firms were becoming comfortable with their position of people-intensive systems, rather than computer-based self-service. Though some executives may think that labor-intensive systems will prevail, they are leaving a huge opening in the market for their competitors. Self-service strategies have proven their worth and will be used for years to come. Both new and renewed companies will embrace the concept in a big way and portals will be one of the primary vehicles that allow firms to implement their self-service strategy.

Leveraging core competency

While many talk of a return to core competencies in the enterprise, developing the strategy to make this occur requires more than words. The primary assets in any operation are the people. In order to really leverage these resources, the information sources and systems that surround them need to be enhanced.

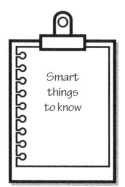

"The main armament in any successful business is the staff of the organization."

Partners.com – Courtesy, Michael J. Cunningham, Perseus Book Group 2001

A recent IDC survey (see below) indicated how important leveraging these skills and systems has become. Many organizations cannot gain this leverage unless the technology is externalized to those that need it. For example, what is the use of an inventory-management system, if the sales staff of your partners do not have access to it? Leveraging the core competencies of the operation means redistributing information to those that need it, and delivering it at the right time. Supply-chain applications are another very important candidate for this work, where the status of products, configuration controls, and time-to-market all have a huge impact on the success of the business. Linking these systems together, so that the customer, product and distribution systems are combined in a relevant form is a key to success. This will then improve business practices and the business decisions made around them. Portal technology again helps dramatically in these efforts.

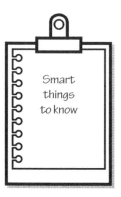

PERCENTAGE OF SYSTEMS FULLY INTEGRATED WITH WEB DESKTOPS

CRM	18%
ERP	26%
Supply chain	14%
Order processing	23%

Source: International Data Corp.

While gluing the relevant applications together in a common framework may seem an obvious move for executives who want to leverage the knowledge that is littered around the organization, there are other places where "low-hanging fruit" is also rife. The myriad of departmental intranets that now dominate medium- and large-scale operations can be a diamond in the rough. Many of these systems have very important and relevant information, but are only accessible to a few. By using portal technology, executives and CIOs are weaving together relevant information sources from the intranet and beyond. Combining search tools with portal solutions allows organizations to share content and collaborate much more effectively. In a world where we continue to drown in data, portal technologies offer a means to provide sanity and simpler navigation to achieve information sharing.

Smart
things
to know

> Leveraging the skills and systems inside the organization will be a key method to create value for that organization's future.

Knowledge-management applications and collaborative systems, ranging from email to wireless applications, provide the foundation for how many operations have to work together. Sharing this information and providing tools that will allow "natural collaboration" to occur among workgroups will be key to success. The simplification of data access is one element that has made portal technology less susceptible to IT cuts, (according to a recent *Information Week* study). This is mainly because many of the projects are relatively inexpensive and can be implemented in short periods of time, compared with many other enterprise initiatives. By leveraging existing systems, whether CRM, manufacturing or other information repositories, portal technology can assist operations to leverage the information by finding and delivering it to those in need.

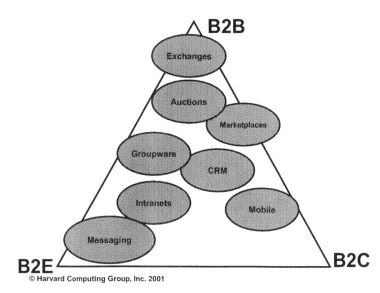

Fig. 8.2 The leverage of existing systems in a common framework creates improved performance for many organizations.

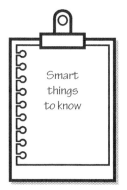

WHAT CORPORATIONS WANT FROM PORTAL TECHNOLOGIES

They want them to:

- unify business applications;
- provide dynamic content;
- allow employee customization; and
- provide simplified access to corporate data.

Source: Harvard Computing Group, Inc.

Ability to adapt to changing business conditions

Perhaps the biggest challenge for many organizations today is to be ready for another storm. In general, executives understand that they have to be ready to deal with change, but many organizations are not truly ready. Often it is the IT systems and the knowledge-sharing mechanisms that are least ready to deal with rapid change.

In the creation of a change-ready environment, many are now turning to new strategies in the development and use of technology. Given that the statistics of failure (outlined earlier) are so daunting, learning methods to reduce risk almost becomes mandatory for executives and managers around the globe.

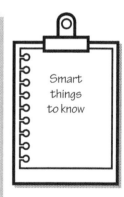

BEST PRACTICES IN PORTAL TECHNOLOGIES

If you want to apply best practices, do the following:

- design systems based on roles not individuals;
- single sign-on to maintain security and control;
- include personalization and customization in the requirements; and
- include portal technologies in solution to leverage existing and new sources of information.

Source: Harvard Computing Group, Inc.

Business-ready systems

The concept of *business ready systems* is a new one. Based on the increasing requirements of demanding technology change, market movements and the need to respond to them, a "ready for change" approach is one way of anticipating change and being prepared for it. There is a good reason that some firms are just better at adapting to changing business environments. They embrace change, they are ready for it, and the really smart ones enjoy change. In the technology selection and adoption curve, careful planning that allows organizations to select tools that are flexible and adaptable makes it easier to deal with new needs as they arise. In addition, systems that allow an organization to rapidly develop and deploy tools also make a huge difference to their flexibility. This allows the operation to be responsive to changing business conditions, and not to miss opportunities. As organizations juggle the priorities for their IT initiatives and spending, many make portal technologies their top priority. As a result, they maximize the return on investment for many other IT implementations by leveraging the portal as an infrastructure assisting in the deployment of multiple applications.

Executives need not be technology wizards in order to use these guidelines to improve the odds of success. Taking advantage of portal systems that base access and information delivery on the profile of a worker's role, rather than on the specific needs of the individual, can make it much more flexible and cost-effective. Technologies such as "single sign-on" can save thousands of hours in password fumbling and support. Portal solutions, deployed with such features, allow individuals to sign on once to the portal, and the underlying technology takes care of enabling access to all the relevant systems and information resources. Many firms now understand how important it is to incorporate personalization and customization capabilities into their systems, if only to be ready to change when the opportunity either presents or demands it.

Planning for change means picking technologies that can change rapidly when you need to change. Most Web and portal technology has some level of customization to allow individual groups to change the way that data and applications are accessed and presented when necessary.

Business drivers have to lead the technology

The days are upon us when business drivers will start to take the high ground on large-scale systems and technology decisions. The stakes are becoming too high for the organization that is not leveraging either its skills or its staff. Building good business cases to drive the requirements for portals and other technologies is likely to be a foundation skill for the future, and not an exception to the rule. Return on investment will be a common theme to many projects in the coming years and months. The following are basic examples of where an organization can look for the business cases to achieve significant ROI.

Executives need to fully understand what these technologies can do for them, and what the impact on their business will be if they "wait for it to happen around them." The competitive edge will go to those that understand and exploit these technologies.

A few years ago I registered the domain name www.technologyforbusiness.com. (This was with a view that most businesses will eventually start looking at technology as an asset they need to control, not as an overhead.) I still believe that "business-driven technology decisions" *will* become a trend. However, the amount of time that this has taken to take hold in the market is astonishing. On a daily basis, companies are still making technology selections before their business model or work processes are analyzed and tested. Then we wonder why so much change and anguish has occurred in the marketplace.

This change will have to come from within. To quote an earlier quip in the book, "Don't try and teach a pig to sing ..." Businesses have to wake up and smell the roses, and if we want to grow them, we have to use the sound principles that were there before the Internet and will remain in place as it becomes mainstream.

Flexibility, agility, and our ability to change rapidly are not just about attitude. This may be the foundation, but systems and tools, and processes also have to be flexible; without this we may know that we need to change things, but do not have the means to change them.

Taking these next steps will bring us to the realization that the Internet, and its surrounding technologies are building blocks for our future: ones we can choose to use, or wait to see what our competitors decide for us. It may not make the difference between whether we have a business or not, but it certainly will impact how efficient and profitable it is.

Recommended Reading

Blown to Bits, Philip Evans and Thomas S Wurster, Harvard Business School Press.

Blur: The Speed of Change in the Connected Economy, Christopher Meyer, Stan Davis, Capstone.

Customers.Com, Patricia B. Seybold Times Books.

Cyber Rules: Strategies for Excelling at E-Business, Thomas M. Siebel, Doubleday.

D2D – Dinosaur to Dynamo: How 20 Established Companies are winning in the New Economy, David Stauffer, Capstone.

Digital Capital: Harnessing the Power of Business Webs, Don Tapscott, David Ticoll, Alex Lowy, Harvard Business School Press.

Enterprise One to One, Peppers and Rogers, DoubleDay.

Flash of Brilliance, William Miller, Perseus Books.

Inside the Tornado, Geoffery Moore, Harper Business.

Net Worth, John Hagel, Marc Singer, Harvard Business School Press.

Net.gain, John Hagel, Arthur G. Armstrong, Harvard Business School Press.

NetSuccess, Christina Ford Haylock, Len Muscarella, Adams Media Corporation.

The Customer Revolution, Patricia Seybold, (Ronni T. Marshak), Jeffrey M. Lewis, Crown Publications.

The Fifth Discipline, Peter M. Senge, DoubleDay.

The X-Economy, Thomas M. Koulopoulos, Nathaniel Palmer, Texere.

Other books by Michael J. Cunningham

B2B: How to Build a Profitable E-Commerce Strategy, Perseus Books, November 2000.

Partners.com: How to Profit from the New DNA of Business, Perseus Book, July 2001.

Glossary

Access provider A company that provides connectivity to the Internet. Customers of access providers pay a fee and are then granted access to the Internet through an electronic account defined and managed by the providers.

Active-X Multimedia extensions for Web browsers provided by Microsoft Corporation to improve Web-site browsing experience.

Asymmetric Digital Subscriber Line (ADSL) Provides high-bandwidth connections to the Internet, but uses twisted copper wiring so that regular phone lines can be used. Bellcore Labs in New Jersey initially developed this cost-effective method of bringing bandwidth to homes and small businesses in 1993.

Andreessen, Marc Marc Andreessen led the team that created Netscape Navigator through his company, Mosaic Communications Corporation.

Before creating Netscape Navigator, Andreessen created NCSA Mosaic at the National Center for Supercomputing applications.

ARPANET (Advanced Research Projects Agency Network)   The first Internet, developed in the 1960s as a way for US authorities to communicate with each other in the aftermath of a nuclear attack. This formed the basis of what has subsequently evolved into today's Internet.

Authentication   The name of the process to verify the identity of a user as they log onto a network.

Bandwidth   Bandwidth describes the amount of data that can travel through the Internet or communications network in a specific period of time. This is usually measured in seconds.

Berners-Lee, Tim   While working in Geneva, Switzerland at CERN, the European Particle Physics Laboratory, Berners-Lee created the World Wide Web.

Bookmarks   Provides the user with the ability to mark their favorite pages and Web sites so that they may be accessed quickly and easily. Most browsers support the bookmark function.

Bricks and mortar   A term used to describe traditional stores and methods of selling and distributing products. Barnes and Noble who sell books through their stores as well as on-line can be described of using both bricks-and-mortar and e-commerce strategies in their business.

Brochureware   The act of putting your corporate literature in basic static form directly to a Web site. Often bores visitors to death, and causes rapid exits from the site.

Browser   A software application, (such as Netscape Communicator and Microsoft Internet Explorer), which interprets the HTML and Web documents so that they may operate on a point-and-click interface. A browser can be used to run complete software applications with extensions and plug-ins.

Bulletin Board System (BBS)   This system allows others to read, comment and electronically post new messages to the group reading them. Often used for interest groups, customer support or professional groups, BBS systems represent a low-cost and effective collaboration forum for the Internet.

Business-to-business (B2B)   The portion of the Internet market that affects transactions between business operations and their partners in marketing, sales, development, manufacturing and support. The largest portion of the Internet marketplace, and the fastest growing.

Channels   Can have two meanings in the Internet. A "channel" is a Web site designed to deliver content from the Internet to your computer, similar to subscribing to a favorite Web site. Typically, it is not necessary to subscribe the Web, but by connecting to the "channel" suggested content can be delivered to your desktop browser.

Channels of distribution   A distribution channel is a method of providing your product or service to the target user of the system. This could be an on-line mall, portal, your own brand site or distribution supply chain.

Change management   The program to define, implement and refine the changes required for the business to affect a change in strategy, process and technology. Used extensively in existing bricks-and-mortar firms to assist staff to transition to new business practices.

Chat Chat systems are used to allow users of networks and the Internet to communicate in real time. Messages today are typically posted via a desktop window with other members of the group. The message will then appear in the open chat windows of others in that particular group for review and further comment.

Click-and-mortar Organizations that have bricks-and-mortar (traditional non-Internet-based) businesses that have changed their strategies to provide both on-line and off-line channels for their clients and business partners.

Click-thru The act of clicking (with a mouse) on a particular graphic or element on a Web-page. Click-thrus are measured to determine the effectiveness of advertising, content and traffic patterns of individual Web sites.

Communicator Netscape's browser, collaboration, and communication software developed in January 1997.

Community Electronic forum where individuals and groups gather to find relevant and pertinent information. They are often segmented by interest or geography.

Content The actual material, text, graphics and other multimedia that make up a Web site.

Content management The system and method by which content is updated, changed and re-posted to the Web site.

Cookie Stores personal preferences for Internet information and communication tools in files in a browser's folder. A text file that contains the information of user's preferences is created and is stored in memory while the browser is running. In addition to personal preferences, cookies can also save information such as the date that the Web site was visited, what purchases were made, what ad banners were clicked on, what files were downloaded, and the information viewed.

CPM (cost per thousand) impressions A measurement of how many times someone has viewed your banner ad via a browser.

Customer Relationship Management Technology systems and internal processes to support the continuous relationship with clients from early stage prospecting through to customer support. Typically provide support for sales, marketing, support, finance and, increasingly, workflow processes to allow clients to serve themselves with information and product.

Cyberspace Coined by William Gibson in 1984, this term is used to describe the place where people interact, communicate, and exchange information using the Internet

Dial-Up Networking Allows a PC to dial into their server and connect to the Internet using either SLIP (Serial Line Interface Protocol) or PPP(Point-to-Point Protocol) connections. The connection makes it possible for the user to work with any software that supports the communication protocol TCP/IP groups, in which hosts and local area networks are placed.

Disintermediation Being excluded from a business network or supply chain due to new market conditions, pricing or distribution process and operations. Usually happens when the value being provided by the organization is not high enough to prevent getting squeezed out of the chain.

Domain   All of the computer users of a commercial Internet provider make up a domain.

Domain name   The unique name that is used to identify a Web site. It contains two or more parts separated by a dot. The existing domain names fit into one of seven categories: educational institutions; commercial organizations; military; government; non-profit organizations; networking organizations; and international organizations (e.g. www.capstone.co.uk).

Early adopters   Groups of users and individual that will typically adopt technology and new work processes early in their introduction to the marketplace.

EDI   (Electronic Data Interchange) The controlled transfer of data between businesses and organizations via established security standards.

E-business   Term now used broadly for the act of doing business using the Internet and other electronic means to conduct business.

Email   Electronic mail is the most widely used Internet service. By sending an email, a file is created that will be transmitted and delivered to the electronic mailbox of the person you address. Can also be used to transfer files containing other information such as documents, programs and multimedia data.

Excite   A popular search engine and portal, which uses keywords to create summaries of each of the Web pages and Usenet newsgroups the search criteria matches. Excite is one of the most widely used search engines that provides a full range of services, including a comprehensive subject directory.

Extranets Private wide area networks that run on public protocols with the goal of fostering collaboration and information-sharing between organizations. A feature of extranets is that companies can allow certain guests to have access to internal data on a controlled basis.

E-tailing On-line sales of retail style goods. Many consumer and specialist goods are now available via these on-line e-tailers.

E-zines On-line publications in the form of newsletters or magazines that allow for a new way for communication and interaction to occur on the Internet (e.g. www.salon.com).

FAQ (Frequently Asked Questions) Helpful way for new users to look at questions that are regularly asked, usually saved on a bulletin board or as archived files.

File Server A computer that stores and makes available programs and data available to other computers on a connected network.

Finger A locator used to find people on the Internet. Its most common use is to detect data about a particular user, such as telephone number, whether they are currently logged on, or their email address. The individual being "fingered" must have his or her profile on the mail system, otherwise there may be no results to a finger query.

Firewall A software/hardware combination that separates an internal local area network from the external Internet. This is done for security purposes in order to protect a company's network from the outside world, and unauthorized electronic visitors.

FTP (File Transfer Protocol) A protocol used on the Internet to transfer many different types of information in the form of files and data. These files and data may contain software, text documents, sound, or images. Used as a way of transferring data from one site to another, this protocol is now transparent to many users using browser-based applications.

Gateway A hardware or software component that links two otherwise incompatible applications or networks.

Gopher A navigational tool that finds resources and information on the Internet by using a multi-level menu system. The main menu is a list of hyperlinks, each with an icon that describes the type of resource to which the resource connects. The resources that a hyperlink could be connected to could be a text file, a movie or binary file, an image, or an index.

History of the Internet The Internet was created in the 1960s by the US Department of Defense as a method of sustaining electronic communication after a nuclear attack. The Rand Corporation, the foremost military think tank created the first communication network that has evolved into today's Internet. After ARPANET – the network that connected four US campuses – was a huge success, research continued into the 1970s. Many large organizations and companies created private computer networks. In the 1980s, ARPANET evolved into the Internet due to the TCP/IP protocol. The popularity of personal computers and the increasingly powerful network servers made it possible for companies to connect to the Internet. The Internet has grown in popularity at an incredible pace and Microsoft and Netscape have created browsers with increasingly complicated and sophisticated software, making the Internet more accessible.

Home page Using HTML (hypertext markup language), Internet providers are able to create a home page, which is the first page that a user sees after entering a URL for a Web site. (Now sometimes called the index page).

HTML (Hypertext Markup Language) The language used to create a Web page. It is used to format the text of a document, specify links to other documents and describe the structure of the Web page. In addition to these main uses, HTML may also be used to display different types of media, such as images, video and sound.

HTTP (Hypertext Transfer Protocol) A protocol used to transfer information within the World Wide Web.

Hyperlink An electronic link that can be programmed so that it is possible to make a jump from one document or Web page to another. These are primary tools for navigating the Internet.

Impressions The number of times that an element of a page has been viewed by an individual browser. Often used to count Internet ad placements.

Intranet Internet-based computing networks that are private and secure. Typically used by corporations, government and other organizations, these are based upon Internet standards and provide the means for an organization to make resources more readily available to its employees on-line.

IP (Internet Protocol) Software that divides information into packets. It then transmits this information in its divided form. This is required for all computers on the Internet to communicate.

IP address An address that identifies each computer on the Internet using a string if four sets of numbers separated by periods.

IRC An acronym for Internet Relay Chat. Allows individuals to "chat" on the Internet. *See* Chat.

ISP   Internet Service Providers deliver a wide range of services to individual users and organizations for the Internet. These include Web hosting, electronic mail, FTP, and many other e-commerce services.

ISDN (Integrated Services Digital Network)   A telephone service that has become a popular, cost-effective solution to traditional dial-up speeds over the Internet. ISDN allows ordinary telephone lines to transmit digital instead of analog signals, thereby permitting much faster dial up and transmission speeds.

Internic   Governing body controlling the issuance and control of Internet domains and addresses. Currently a partnership between the US government and Network Solutions, Inc.

IT   Abbreviation for Information Technology.

Java   A programming language that was created in 1995 in order to allow Java programs, to be downloaded and run on a Web browser. Developed by Sun Microsystems, Java is an object-oriented programming language that allows content and software to be distributed through the Internet. Applications that are written in Java much be run by a Java-enabled Web browser.

Kermit   A file transfer program that is popular on mainframe computers.

Killer App (application)   An incredibly useful, creative program that provides a breakthrough for its users. The first killer app of the Internet was email.

LAN (Local Area Network)   A computer network that operates and is located in one specific location. Many of these may be connected together in order to enable users to share resources and information on their network.

Legacy system Generally described as an existing computer system that is providing a function for some part of the business. Often these systems are considered older in nature, but provide some strategic function to the business. Examples include: Inventory Management Systems; Manufacturing Resource Planning systems (MRP); Enterprise Resource Planning (ERP); Sales Automation Systems; and Help Desk Systems.

Listserv mailing lists Listserv is a system that distributes email. It manages interactive mailing lists and can either be controlled by staff or by a computer program. They are used by groups with common interests who want to share information or resources.

MIME (Multipurpose Internet Mail Extension) A standard method to identify the type of data contained in a file based on its extension. MIME is an Internet protocol that allows you to send binary files across the Internet as attachments to email messages. These files includes graphics, programs, sound and video files, as well as electronic office files. MIME allows different types of systems to interpret these different files types successfully.

Mirroring Exact copying of the content of one computer disk to another. Used to back-up information in mission critical systems, and permit the maintenance of others while the system is still running.

Moore's Law Gordon E. Moore, co-founder of Intel, said in 1965 that he predicted that the processing power of integrated circuits would double every 18 months for the next ten years. This law has proven true for almost 30 years and is now used in many performance forecasts. Moore's second law is that the cost of production would double every generation.

Multimedia   Term used to describe many different forms of media being used for particular applications. Multimedia applications often include, graphics, animation, sound and video elements.

Navigator   Term used to refer to Netscape Navigator, the browser created by Netscape Communications Corporation (formally known as Mosaic Communications Corporation), first released in October 1994.

Newsgroup   An electronic discussion group comprising of collections of postings to particular topics. These topics are posted to server designated as a the news server for this group. Newsgroups can be an invaluable source of information when trying to resolve problems and get advice.

Newsreader   A software program that lets you subscribe to newsgroups, in addition to reading and posting messages to them. Will keep track of groups visited and favorites for simplified navigation when returning and tracking activities in different groups.

Net   Term used to refer to the Internet.

Netiquette   Set of rules that users are encouraged to follow if participating in an electronic discussion group or sending email on the Internet

NIH   Abbreviation for Not Invented Here.

Node   An individually addressable point on a network. Could be a computer, printer or server on the network.

One-to-one marketing   Customization and personalization of both product and prospect requirements to meet an individual set of established needs. Once matched, a one-to-one marketing program delivers an exact marketing message, with the appropriate product to meet the prospects needs.

Packet   Term used to describe data being transferred over a network in a unit.

Switching   A communications paradigm used to minimize latency and optimize the use of bandwidth available in a network. It does this by individually routing a packet between hosts using the most expedient route. Once the packets are sent, the destination computer reassembles the packets into their appropriate sequence

Password   A secret word or code that is used to log on to a network. The system checks the word and, if approved, the user has access to the network.

Peer-to-peer   Technology that allows (Internet-based) computer systems to reference information on many other computers without data being local to a specific machine. This allows for massive networks of information to be created without changing the storage location.

PDA (Personal Digital Assistant)   Theses are used to provide relevant computer functions to the individual without the overhead of a laptop or local computer. These now include email, contact information, paging, Web browsing and access to remote corporate applications.

Personalization   Customization of Web information to specifically meet the needs and desires of the individual user.

Plug-In   By extending the standard capabilities of a Web browser, the plug-in permits the running of other programs and many multimedia applications through the Web browsers.

POP (Point of Presence)   Where the Internet server is located.

Portal   Major visiting center for Internet users. The very large portals started life as search engines, AltaVista, AOL, CompuServe, Excite, Infoseek, Lycos, Magellan, and Yahoo! are examples of major portals. B2B portals offer locations for individual business transactions to occur specific to affinity groups and business needs.

PPP (Point-to-Point Protocol)   Internet communication protocol for transferring network data over serial point-to-point links.

Pull Technology   Describes the type of technology used in the Internet, where users searching for and requesting information to be downloaded to their computer.

Push Technology   Delivery of information to potential consumers via electronic means. Often involves the automated transmission of new data on particular topic on a regular basis, or some predetermined event.

Quality of service   Defines the level of service for an individual, voice, data or video connection when using a telecommunications supplier.

RealVideo   Technology that allows users to see video as it is being downloaded.

Redirectors   Programs that send visitors to one segment of a Web site to a new location automatically.

Replication Describes the process of controlled copying of certain elements of a Web site, database or other collection of information. A technique that can provide portions of a system to be automatically distributed to the area that needs it for performance or other reasons.

ROM (read-only memory) A memory chip that stores data concerning instructions and data included at the time of manufacture that cannot easily be changed.

Robot A robot is a program that is designed to automatically go out and explore the Internet for a specific purpose. Some robots record and index all of the contents of the network to create a searchable database, these robots are called spiders.

Router A system at the intersection of two networks that works to determine which path is most efficient for data when traveling to its destination.

Search Directories Subject indexes on the Web that allow users to search for information by entering a keyword into a query box on their site. The directory searches through keyword matches in their database only.

Search Engines Search World Wide Web site, Usenet newsgroups, and other Internet resources to match descriptor words. Many also rank the matches in order of relevancy, making it easier for the user to know what sites are likely to be most helpful.

Server A software program that functions in a client-server information exchange model whose function is to provide information and execute functions for computers attached to the network.

Shareware   Software that is made available to users, by the developers, at no cost. Manufacturers of shareware often ask users to review the applications and sometimes request a fee of $10–25. Shareware is available on Web sites, such as www.jumbo.com; www.shareware.com; and www.tucows.com

SMTP (Simple Mail Transport Protocol)   The protocol for Internet email, where the host name of the Internet provider's mail server must be designated in order to send mail.

Spam   The practice of sending email or posting messages for purely commercial gain, often to very large groups of uninterested users.

Spider   A program designed to browse the Internet and look for information to add to a search tool's database.

Spoofing   Slang for someone impersonating another on the Internet. Typically used in electronic mail applications.

Streaming   Where a plug-in is used to watch a video in real time as it is downloaded, instead of having to store it as a file.

Stickiness   A general term to describe the characteristics of a Web site to attract and keep users in the area. Also a measurement of how many users return to the site for more information or products.

Synchronous Communication   Simultaneous communication using applications such as Internet Streaming, Relay Chat, net phone and video conferencing where communication occurs at the same time.

Subscribe   Term used to describe the act of requesting a subscription to a listserv mailing list.

Targeted marketing   Development of marketing programs by identifying segments in specific markets and designing the product or service to specifically meet these needs.

Templates   Pre-defined application components that allow rapid development and deployment of computer-based systems.

T1 line   A high-speed digital connection that can transmit data at a rate of 1.5 million bps (bits per second). Often used by small and medium size organizations, very fast file transfers to can be made using this type of connection.

T3 line   A very high-speed connection capable of transmitting data at a rate of 45 million bits per second. Good enough to transmit real time video, this type of connection is usually reserved for large organizations.

TCP/IP (Transmission Control Protocol/Internet Protocol)   Set of protocols that allow computers of any make or model to communicate with each other over the Internet. TCP packages the data to be sent and IP provides the addressing information about where the packages are to be sent.

Telnet   Allows users to log onto different computers and run resident programs. Although this is not as lauded as the World Wide Web and requires commands to navigate, it is essential for Internet travel.

Tunneling   A secure mechanism to allow transmission of data across points of access on the Internet.

URL (Uniform Resource Locator)   The standard form for addresses on the Internet that provide the addressing system for other Internet

Virus A program created to cause problems on the computer systems they invade. Virus protection has become a major component in maintaining the health of computer systems everywhere.

Veronica An acronym for Very Easy Rodent Oriented Netwide Index to Computerized Archives, Veronica is a network utility that lets individuals search all of the 6000-plus Gopher servers in the world.

Virtual Private Networks Private networks that allow users to purchase bandwidth and access, often through their Internet connection, without the need to purchase dedicated network cabling or systems.

VRML (Virtual Reality Modeling Language) Language that allows users to experience a simulated three dimensional environment on the computer. This was first developed for video games and now has advanced, creating a non-profit VRML consortium with more than 50 companies.

WAIS An acronym for Wide Area Information Servers, WAIS is a network information retrieval that allows searching for keywords or phrases. These are indexed in special files. Unlike Gopher, WAIS searches the full text of files that it indexes, thereby providing a much larger group of documents for the user to select. This method is the most popular method used by large search engines on the Web.

Wallets Electronic wallets offer the ability for shoppers on the Internet to automatically debit their accounts using e-money. The wallet contains electronic money which is usually deposited in advance, and is replenished as the account needs it. This is likely to become a more common form of shopping in the future.

WAN (Wide Area Network) Made up of local networks that are connected to other local networks by high-speed telephone lines.

Web Server   A server that is connected to the Internet that contains World Wide Web documents.

Whiteboard   The electronic equivalent to a chalkboard, whiteboards provide visual communication and interaction over networks.

Wired   Term used to describe users who are attached to their computers or use the computer and the Web as in integral part of their lifestyle.

World Wide Web   A collection of protocols and standards that makes it possible to view and retrieve information from the Internet. By being linked together in a hypermedia system, this information can be used through the World Wide Web.

WYSIWYG (What You See Is What You Get)   Term used to refer to text and graphics that will print in the same format that it is seen on the screen.

XML   Extensible Markup Language describes the format, presentation, and provides application control over the content, of the documents and systems using this language. Much more powerful than HTML, XML is likely to be the next generation language for the Web and business applications.

Index

Printed and bound by CPI Group (UK) Ltd, Croydon, CR0 4YY

13/04/2025

14656568-0001